MW00943607

Sing to the Seed
Nurturing Our True Nature

MICHAEL HARRIS

www.singtotheseed.com

For my wife and children, with you my heart is home.
In loving memory of Erma, a genuine wisdom mother.
With immense gratitude for Bardor Tulku Rinpoche.
May all beings realize their true nature.

CONTENTS

INTRODUCTION

> The seeds are invisible. They sleep
> in the secrecy of the ground until one
> of them decides to wake up.
> — *Antoine de Saint-Exupéry,*
> *The Little Prince*

A HEARTY SEED SPROUTS effortlessly when the conditions are right. So too will the wakefulness sleeping in the ground of our true nature. The vital factor in this unfolding is connecting with compassion vast enough to cherish the well-being of every being. It is said that such boundless compassion is not only the seed of complete awakening, it is the life-giving water that helps the seed grow, and the fruit that ripens into unshakeable happiness.

The heartfelt aspiration to connect with this kind of compassion unleashed radical change in my own life. At the time I was successful by most conventional measures. Through a mix of hard work and good luck, I had built a thriving research and publishing business in the growing Internet industry. My phone was ringing with calls from reporters at the *New York Times* and *Wall Street Journal* seeking expert insight. Speaking invitations for international conferences arrived regularly, as did research en-gagements with some of the world's leading technology companies.

While I was genuinely grateful for the opportunities and accolades—and my marriage to a wonderful wom-an—I had not found anything resembling unshakeable happiness. Enormous dissatisfaction brewed beneath the surface. Connecting with the truth of this subterranean suffering, I sought a solution through deep spiritual in-quiry and practice, primarily in the Buddhist tradition.

While the road was rocky at times, I eventually met my principal spiritual teacher, an exceptional and icono-clastic woman named Erma Pounds. She was born in 1925 to a family of Irish immigrants in a tiny town along the banks of the Ohio River. Erma's father, an engineer and adept spiritual teacher in his day, started her contempla-tive training at age seven. Erma moved to Phoenix as a young mother to aid the health of her children and began guiding a group of sincere seekers in 1951.

Appreciated as a gifted seer, Erma forged close con-nections with a number of American Indian spiritual elders in the Southwest. She was a confidant of Oswald "White Bear" Fredericks—the progressive Hopi mystic who provided source material to Frank Waters for *The Book of the Hopi*—and of traditional Hopi elders, includ-ing Grandmother Caroline Tawangyama. Following a personal visit to her home in 1974 by one of Tibet's foremost Buddhist masters, the 16th Gyalwang Karmapa

Ranjung Rigpe Dorje, Erma also served as a teacher in the Karmapa's lineage until her death in 2011.

With Erma I was unexpectedly immersed in an old-school spiritual apprenticeship. It was an incredible gift. Passionately nonsectarian, Erma walked her talk through a life of selfless service. Drawing upon a variety of wisdom traditions she relentlessly reminded her students that authentic spirituality aims to cultivate awareness of the truth already present within each of us.

Through Erma I was blessed to connect with Bardor Tulku Rinpoche. A heart-disciple of the 16th Karmapa and a respected Tibetan Buddhist teacher in his own right, Rinpoche also met Erma on the 1974 trip. They remained close friends for more than three decades.

Because Erma's radical teaching style could confuse some orthodox Buddhists, Rinpoche occasionally received questions from disoriented students asking whether she was the real deal. During a public lecture he once made a special effort to dispel any confusion about this by point-ing to the respect his teacher, the 16th Karmapa, displayed for her during their visit. "I think we can infer from his behavior on that occasion that Erma must have been pretty damn special," Rinpoche chuckled.

Before her death Erma asked me if I would lead the community she established. With Rinpoche's encourage-ment, I accepted the role. I had the privilege to serve as the director of both a nonsectarian Buddhist center and affiliated interfaith friendship circle in Arizona for the next five years.

Prior to Erma's passing my wife and I embraced a parallel path as adoptive and foster parents. The journey has been one of the most intense, challenging, and rewarding experiences of our lives.

To help our children I expanded my research interests to include neuroscience and developmental psychology. Encountering the vast body of work on attachment theory—the science of infant-parent bonding—was like being hit on the head by Newton's apple. Besides aiding our family, what I learned serendipitously enriched my spiritual practice and approach to helping others with theirs. It became clear that how we are nurtured profoundly influences the journey of recognizing our true nature.

While compassion is the seed of awakening, devotion to an authentic spiritual lineage acts as a natural form of Miracle Gro. This kind of devotion is the polar opposite of blind faith. Genuine devotion encompasses the yearning to fully connect with our awakened nature, a radical openness to truth, and the courage to confront delusion for the benefit of all. It is taught that practicing without devotion to our unlimited potential—as well as the teachers and teachings that nurture it—is like planting a burnt seed and expecting it sprout.

This is no small challenge. Many of us grow up in a breeding ground for mistrust and resentment. Feeling burned by our early experience with religion and family, we may reflexively recoil from something that seems similar. On the flip side, with idiotic devotion, we can blindly gobble up whatever we meet in a desperate attempt to connect with what we feel is lacking.

Remarkably, the natural world teaches us that a burned seed is essential for the development of some plants. California's giant sequoia—the world's largest tree—depends on the heat of wildfire to crack its thick cones, release seeds for germination, and clear space for the seedlings to develop. Similarly, the experience of being seared by our life experience may ignite a burning desire to find a sustainable solution to suffering.

Through the years I have encountered many books that have offered insights and encouragement. My wish is this book offers that to you. May these words sing to the seed of awakening in all beings, nurturing the recognition of our unchanging true nature.

CHAPTER 1

Cultivating Awareness

"You're talking about a search for the
meaning of life?" I asked. "No, no, no,"
he said. "For the experience of being alive."
— *Mythologist Joseph Campbell
responding to journalist Bill Moyers*

WHILE WE MAY WISH for a peaceful walk in the woods the
awakening journey is also a rain dance with our fears and
fixations, lusts and loathings, boredom and loneliness.
With our legs burning from a marathon of spinning and
stomping, the sky opens when we least expect it. Soaked
by a frigid downpour, goosebumps rise on our skin. Wiggling our naked toes in the fresh mud, we touch the ever-present indestructible purity at our core and savor an
actual taste of the freedom the sages sing of.

Then the clouds recede. Under a searing sun in an
empty blue sky the mud we stand on dries and blisters.
Our conditioned reaction is to resent the difference between dampness and drought. We desperately dance for
more rain, hoping to get back to where we thought we

were. As we see our compulsion for what it is, we can let go and relax into a full breath, heartfelt sob, or raucous belly laugh. We connect with heart space vast enough to cherish the ecstatic catastrophe that is the experience of every living being.

Meditation is sometimes misprescribed as a form of sedation. "Try this, it will help you calm down." While calm is a common and pleasant side effect of the practice, meditation is also like being doused with a cold bucket of water, waking us up to the truth of our actual condition. The Tibetan word for meditation is *gom*, which simply means to cultivate familiarity.

As we become familiar with the workings of our mind we are likely to find it appears to be anything but calm. The point isn't simply to chill out and take the edge off. The essence of meditation is awareness. With sustained practice we become acutely aware of our direct experience, and ultimately, unborn awareness itself.

When we genuinely relax and befriend what we meet an awesome recognition awakens. Within the torrent of our thoughts, feelings, and perceptions is boundless space. Connecting with this fresh expanse we naturally remain open to the intensity of our experience with a sense of kindness and welcoming.

Children often grace us with visceral views into our unconscious grown-up habits. At the park with my second-grader, one of his friends started getting worked up about the idea of leaving in a few minutes. "You need to calm down," the boy's father warned. "You need to breathe."

"Uh, dad," the boy replied with an eye roll, "I am breathing."

Chuckling on the inside, I prodded: "But are you *aware* you are breathing?"

The boy stopped in his tracks.

"Did you know we breathe more than 20,000 times each day? How many of those breaths are you aware of?" I asked.

"We really breathe that much?" his dad asked in disbelief.

Really. His son grinned from ear to ear.

There is an old story about a young man who wanted to learn to meditate. He heard a revered teacher lived in a nearby village, so he walked there to seek instructions. "Go sit in the shade of that tree," the meditation teacher advised. "Rest naturally with your spine straight but not stiff, and watch your breath. When thoughts, feelings, and sensations arise, let each be as it is, and maintain awareness of the breath."

The student marched over to the tree and began practicing with gusto. A few minutes later he returned to the teacher, clearly irritated. "What's the point of this?" he asked. "Watching my breath is so boring."

"Ah," the teacher responded. "Come with me. I have another approach that is more interesting."

They walked together to a nearby stream. "Kneel down and watch your reflection in the water," the teacher said. As the young man gazed at himself in the brook, the teacher grabbed him by the scruff of the neck and plunged his head underwater. Once the teacher released his grip, the young man thrust his head skyward gasping for air.

"Do you still believe the breath is boring?" the teacher asked wryly. "Now go back and sit under the tree."

My own meditation teacher was an extraordinary, and at times ornery, great-grandmother named Erma Pounds. The cantankerousness was but one facet of an immense love for her students. When comfort and support were needed, she let it flow. If a swift kick in the behind was called for, she wouldn't hesitate to lace up her boots.

"Begin your practice with awareness of the breath," she often counseled when asked for meditation instructions. "If you want to meet a master of the breath, go sit with a sleeping baby. Right now, see that baby in your mind's eye. Watch her tiny belly rise with the in-breath and fall with the out-breath. Now, observe the way you are breathing. Are you breathing like that baby or has your natural process inverted?"

Invariably, someone noticed he was breathing backward, his belly contracting and chest expanding with the in-breath. "Relax," she encouraged. "Breathe naturally. Inhale, belly out; exhale belly in. So much suffering in this world results from our forgetting how to breathe naturally."

Research from a range of scientific disciplines concurs. Inverted breathing is a sign that our body is in a stress state and the list of possible adverse effects for our physical and psychological health is long. Interestingly, however, research also illuminates that external stressors are not our problem, per se. It is our resistance to and fear of stressors that helps turn them toxic. In other words, our relationship with what is happening deeply matters.

In the human experience, resistance—and the suffering that arises from it—can be summed up with one letter: I. More precisely, the viscerally felt sense of "I" seeking to defend or expand its territory. Sometimes this vividly appearing I is called "ego" within contemplative spiritual traditions. However, the meaning differs from the ego described in the psychological domain.

Psychologically, ego refers to a foundational sense of self or personality that enables us to function. Spiritually speaking, ego (as the visceral I) describes a pattern of I-centricity or self-preoccupation that becomes a catalyst for dissatisfaction and suffering.

To be clear that we are referring to this visceral sense of I, me, or mine identified contemplatively, let's use a unique term for it: the igo. (We now live in a world full of ipads, tunes, and clouds, after all).

The igo is selfie mind. It is obsessed with what "I do" and where "I go." It operates along an axis of grasping and aversion, desperately hoping for pleasure, praise, fame, and gain while fearing their opposites: the experience of pain, blame, insignificance, and loss. The igo's discontent is not constrained to real-time experience—its ruminations and agitations about the past and future flood the present. Nor does the igo hesitate to turn upon itself with an inflated sense of eminence or inadequacy.

The key to the igo's power is our ignorance of its actual nature. With open-mindedness, kind-heartedness, and a sense of humor, investigate the pattern in your direct experience. When in the igo's grip, pause and look. Trace your thoughts and feelings back to their roots. In the final accounting, doesn't it all come down to either a strong sense of "I want" or "I don't want" a particular object, experience, or self-perception? The igo reacts and we go along for the ride.

After work, you drive to the local supermarket. As you pull into the parking lot, you eye a prime parking space close to the entrance. The only other available space is on the far end of the lot. As the frigid weather turns blustery and rainy, you realize your coat and umbrella are back at the office. The perceived value of that up-front parking space is skyrocketing. Just as you are about to pull into that attractive spot, another car zips in. The igo leaps into action.

"How dare that jackass steal my parking space!"

In a heartbeat, the igo has taken personal possession of a piece of asphalt marked by two white lines owned by a grocery store. Unsatisfied, the igo then morphs into a judge and jury. Its verdict: the driver of the other vehicle is actually a mule.

Unimpeded, the igo continues expanding into the equivalent of an omniscient iGod. Yes, the igo believes it can clearly perceive every conceivable cause and condition throughout the infinite flow of space-time that led to this precise moment and confidently proclaim: "I am right! They are wrong! They stole it from me!" Undaunted, the igo seals the deal by blaming itself: "And it's because I didn't act quickly enough! I screwed up."

The door of the other car opens. An elderly man in a raincoat steps out from the driver's seat. He waddles to the rear of the car, opens the trunk, pulls out a wheel chair, and rolls it to the passenger door for his wife. Once she is safely on board, he offers a thank you wave, pointing to the row of adjacent handicapped parking spaces that are all occupied.

So exactly who is the jackass? Seriously. Who or what is this igo that so fiercely wants or doesn't want what is actually happening? Can you find it? Go on, take a look.

Any luck yet?

No? Keep searching.

Still can't find anything?

Well done. You are better off trying to catch water with a net. The igo is a phantom, a mirage. It cannot be found in one place within our body or outside of it. It has no shape, color, or texture. It has no measurable weight, length, or volume.

The igo is like an inner Wizard of Oz, speaking with a booming voice, hoping we will never peer behind the curtain and learn the truth. And yet, like an obedient dog, we unquestioningly follow the igo's proclamations and commands. Unconsciously identifying with igo casts a shadow on our true nature, obscuring our innate capacity for compassion, wisdom, and skillful action.

We are all in the same boat here on Earth. Careening through an expanse of lifeless space at 70,000 miles per hour we take an annual trip together around the sun. Every one of us on this big blue-green marble wishes to be free of suffering and live in happiness. Who can honestly claim to have a greater inherent right to the fulfilment of that aspiration? The igo relentlessly makes its case.

Ultimately, igo gone wild is the root cause of every serious threat we face to life on this planet—from climate change and war to inequities in the availability of basic necessities. Any genuinely sustainable solution for our well-being must include liberating our relationship with this illusory inner beast and buffoon.

The igo has a fabled history. In the Judeo-Christian parable of our beginnings, Adam and Eve live in blissful harmony with Creator and Creation in the Garden of Eden. That is until they take a bite from an apple that falls from the tree of knowledge (of the igo). Self-preoccupation is born.

"What the heck? I am naked! And I feel ashamed of it!" the igo laments.

"Get out of here you menace! Be gone!" the Creator bellows.

"You're right. I should go. I am unworthy," the igo whimpers as it limps away from paradise.

The igo doesn't get that the Creator loves Creation as it is—so much so in fact—that the Almighty is willing to powerfully cut through the delusion of separateness and self-fixation. This forthrightness hurts the igo's feelings. It craves validation.

In our ever expanding iworld, many businesses thrive by enabling "frictionless" commerce. In other words, they strive 24/7 to ensure there are no inconveniences when we are ready to buy. Authentic spiritual paths are awakening systems that take the opposite approach: they intentionally inconvenience the igo, squeezing it until it cries uncle. Rather than coddle the igo, the goal is to blaze a trail that leads to freedom from its tyranny.

While my igo would never admit it, what it desperately wanted was a conceptually and emotionally agreeable spiritual path that fit within the confines of its expectations. Instead, my teacher loved me enough to push me outside of my igo's comfort zone again and again.

Not long after I started studying and practicing with Erma, she developed a habit of not showing up for scheduled teachings at the Buddhist center she directed in Arizona. Instead, when I arrived ready to learn, one of Erma's long-time students would relay the message that it would be helpful if I led the meeting in her absence.

"Now walk, dammit," I could almost hear her say. "You know how to do this. Let go of the igo's limitations and take a step from your true nature." Doing so proved to be both excruciating and liberating as layers of conditioning were exposed and progressively untangled. Over time, I found that the further we open into the igo-free zone, the more deeply we connect with love, compassion, joy, and equanimity—and each other.

The point here is not to put tough-love on a pedestal and imply that tenderness is a way of weakness. Quite the opposite is true. In fact, it is a lack of nurturing for the naturally breathing babies in our care that helps create fertile ground for the growth of igo.

CHAPTER 2

Sing to the Seed

The wronging or cherishing of seeds or young plants
is that that is most important to their thriving.
— *Sir Francis Bacon*

DURING ONE OF THE LEARNING opportunities my teacher kindly orchestrated by not showing up, I had the unexpected pleasure of meeting a Crow Indian medicine woman visiting our Buddhist center from Montana. After I had finished leading the evening's meditation, the medicine woman introduced herself. Out of the blue she explained that in her traditional culture, once a woman knows she is pregnant, she begins singing to her unborn child. Through songs of gratitude and celebration a mother welcomes the being-to-be into her body and our world. She sings of the sun and moon, mountains and rivers, plants and animals, to connect her developing child with the complete circle of life.

The medicine woman began to sing to me as a Crow mother would to the human seed growing within her.

Although I could not translate the words of her language, the meaning shared through feeling was crystal clear. Her welcome song offered unconditional acceptance, caring, and joy. In her culture, she later explained, a deep-rooted connection between mother and child is consciously cultivated with awareness of conception, during pregnancy, and in the first years of life.

Rather than simple superstition, we now understand that such traditional ways are instinctually wise. While the igo is a fundamental variable in the human equation, a lack of love and nurturing early in life serves to super-size our suffering self. As our sense of resistance and separation grows, so do impediments to connecting with our true nature.

Research finds that excessive stress experienced by a mother during pregnancy can have long-lasting effects on the baby growing within her. When cortisol levels are elevated in a mother's body, the stress hormone may pass through her placenta and influence the growth of her developing child. High levels of cortisol in the womb correlate with lower measured IQ, birth weight, and a host of potential social-emotional challenges. On the other hand, engagement with music and meditation practices are shown to reduce cortisol levels and boost the release of neurotransmitters that elevate mood and contribute to a feeling of well-being.

Although most of our brain's cells—called neurons— are present at birth only a fraction of the connections among them have been made. More than 80 percent of these links will be formed by age three. Sensitive nurturing stimulates the formation of these essential connections, promoting optimal nervous system integration and functioning. Whether an infant grows to live with a natural sense of openness and empathy, confidence and curiosity, compassion and resilience, is linked to the quality of the connection formed with her primary caregivers. Remarkably, nearly half of us may lack this supportive foundation of early nurturing, known as attachment security.

My wife and I were once invited to attend a weekend of teachings in Portland, Ore. with His Holiness the Dalai Lama focused on the relationship between spirituality and environmental sustainability. To the surprise of the eco-friendly audience, Tibet's spiritual leader pointed to the importance of early childhood caregiving in the equation. Gazing upon the large crowd in the sports arena, the Buddhist monk explained that while everyone there appeared educated and well-off, meaningful differences existed below the surface.

The Nobel Peace Prize recipient shared his understanding that those who receive affection and nurturing early in life seem to have a greater sense of contentment and kindness. By comparison, he explained, those who received less love in early childhood or experienced abuse—no matter how successful they became as adults—deep inside, continue to be haunted by "some sense of insecurity that automatically creates fear and unhappiness." This pain can undermine the expression of our natural compassion, he noted, including the capacity to care for each other and the planet that sustains us.

The Dalai Lama directly spoke to the power of this principle in his own life. Although born into a peasant family in a remote area of Tibet, the Dalai Lama believed he inherited tremendous inner wealth. As his family went about their daily tasks—whether working in the fields or tending to the animals—he was always carried securely on his mother's shoulder and nursed at her breast. The Dalai Lama believed the seeds of compassion that fully blossomed later in his life were sown through the affection he experienced in his earliest years at home and further developed through extensive spiritual training. If the expression of our innate compassion is impeded by painful childhood experience, he counseled, we can still consciously cultivate our capacity for caring.

By highlighting the vital role nurturing plays in the healthy development of children, the intention here is not to place responsibility for it upon the shoulders of mothers alone. As an activity, the mothering or nurturing of a young child is not limited to mothers or women. What is essential is that a capable adult offer the care needed for a baby to forge a secure bond. A father or grandparent, aunt or uncle, adoptive or foster parent, or other substitute caregiver can provide the nurturing a young child needs, offering benefits that last a lifetime.

Siddhartha Gautama, who would later become known as the Buddha, was a beneficiary of such loving kindness from a surrogate. In the ornate account of Prince Siddhartha's birth, it is told that his mother, Queen Mayadevi, died a week after her son was born. Fortunately for Siddhartha, following this profound loss the Queen's sister "raised him with affection, as if he were her own son."

Thirty-five years later Siddhartha would realize complete enlightenment while meditating beneath a fig tree and became known as the Buddha, the awakened one. He understood that just as the tree shading him had matured from a single seed, so too had his own awakening. The Buddha recognized every living being possessed the same potential. He called this primordially pure seed of awakening within us *tathagatagharba*. The spiritual path is not about acquiring something outside us; rather it is a process of weeding out the igo and cultivating conditions for the fruition of the seed of awakening that is already present.

A lack of nurturing early in life can reap a harvest of emotional anguish. It may feel as if our awakening seed is not just concealed within the ordinary muck and mud of life, but paved over with a thick layer of concrete. However, as impenetrable as the igo's artificial barriers appear, the seed of our awakened nature remains unscathed and ready to germinate. When we sing to this seed its potential stirs. Cracks begin to form in seemingly impervious barriers. Light and moisture seep through the dark crevices, and with incredible force, a tender shoot thrusts skyward toward fruition.

THE GRIP OF A NEWBORN'S HAND is so strong that a baby can briefly support her own weight in midair. This powerful primal reflex creates a physical attachment to the mother, as if baby is literally hanging on for dear life. Compared to the warmth and familiarity of the womb, our outer world may seem cold and hostile. It is the presence of a loving caregiver that transforms this space into a warm, safe, and nurturing environment. It is like the difference between living on the inhospitable surface of the moon or within Earth's life-giving atmosphere.

About a year after birth a simple psychological test can measure the quality of the infant-caregiver bond. It foretells whether he may live with a sense of openness and optimism, compassion and connectedness, or is at increased risk to suffer from depression, anxiety, addiction, or even a personality disorder. It is called the Strange Situation Procedure. Here's how it works.

A mother, or another primary caregiver, brings her year-old baby into an observational playroom. The infant is set down and allowed to explore while mom watches. After about 20 minutes, a stranger enters the room, starts a conversation with mom and engages with baby as mom quietly leaves. During this initial separation the stranger maintains a child-centered focus. Mom returns in a few minutes, makes contact with her baby, offers comfort if needed, and leaves. This time the infant is left alone and the stranger is distant. Soon, mom returns, warmly greets and picks up her child as the stranger departs inconspicuously.

It is like a scene you might observe at a daycare center as a mother prepares to leave her little one for the day.

However, in this exercise concocted to provoke separation anxiety, developmental psychologists are carefully observing four aspects of the baby's behavior. First, how does the infant explore the environment: is he confident or timid, curious or disoriented? Second, what is the child's reaction to the departure of his caregiver: is he aware or out to lunch, calm or fearful? Third, how much anxiety does the baby show when left alone with the stranger? And finally, how does the baby behave when reunited with his caregiver? Is he immediately soothed and calmed by his mother's presence, seem shell shocked, or continue to cry inconsolably?

Depending on the behavior observed, the baby is identified as having either a secure or insecure attachment relationship with his primary caregiver. The difference offers clues about how the baby's nervous system is developing, and the way he feels about the world and the people in it.

To survive, every baby forms an attachment. The issue is how the attachment is forged. Is it whole-hearted and secure or conflicted and insecure? A securely-attached baby is bonded with her caregiver in love and trust. As a baby's needs are affectionately and consistently met, she can relax into the pains and pleasures of the human experience.

Insecure attachment arises from an unresolvable conflict in an infant's experience. A baby is innately drawn to his caregiver for the fulfillment of his basic needs. But, when the caregiver does not reliably meet these needs, it is a painful push-pull dynamic that the baby must bridge to survive. To adapt, the developing child learns to repress his own naturally-arising frustration, anger, anxiety, and sadness—or express it in the extreme.

The keys to attachment security are awareness, empathy, affection, and attunement—the ability of a caregiver to "tune in" to her child's needs, preferences, temperament, and personality. The sensitive caregiver can consistently read his baby's needs, even subtle cues, then reliably respond and meet them.

To illustrate the principle in practice, imagine visiting four different restaurants. At your favorite neighborhood bistro, the Caring Café, the waiter warmly greets you by name. Without having to ask, he escorts you to your preferred table—the one by the picture window with a stunning view of the flower garden in full bloom. When returning with the menu, he also delivers an iced tea, your regular drink. You place your order and a delicious meal arrives promptly.

In caring for your needs, he manages to strike the perfect balance—attentive but not hovering, engaging though not imposing. After the meal, when you ask for coffee he delivers it piping hot and leaves enough room for cream, knowing that's the way you like it. The bill arrives when you are finished, and once you pay, the change is returned quickly. You gladly share a generous tip and depart as a thoroughly satisfied and securely attached customer.

The following week you try a different spot, the Clueless Café. A sign instructs customers to seat themselves. After finding a table, you are greeted by a cheerful, upbeat waitress who seems eager to help. Thirsty, you ask for an iced tea. She brings you a beer. Famished, you order a Caesar salad. She brings you a hamburger. Feeling nature's call, you ask for the location of the restroom. With a radiant smile, she points you to a door in the back of the restaurant. Opening it, you enter a supply closet. Even though this waitress is as sweet as can be, are you a happy customer? What if this Clueless Café were the only place to go for food in your town, and the pattern continued day after day, month after month?

Hoping for a better meal, you take a trip to the Cold Café. The waitress here is distant, perhaps even depressed. Your smiles are met with blank stares or sometimes, tears. Your overtures for assistance are ignored. The waitress is so preoccupied with her own suffering it is as if you don't exist. Because your physical and emotional needs are often unmet, here you find yourself feeling confused, alone, afraid, and angry.

The eatery next door, the Cruel Café, is even worse. When you share concerns about your unpleasant experience, the waiter goes ballistic. He blames you for the mistakes, yells at you, and threatens you physically. Sometimes, he snaps and hits you. Other times, he leaves you alone for extended periods while drunk or high as a kite. All the while you are still hungry, thirsty, and desperately need to go to the bathroom. Here you feel terrified and enraged.

Attachment security is on the menu at the Caring Café. The other cafés highlight three insecure attachment types identified through Strange Situation evaluations: 1) *avoidant;* 2) *anxious;* and 3) *disorganized.*

Like the customer in the Clueless Café, an infant forms an *avoidant attachment* by experiencing his caregiver as emotionally detached and dismissing of his needs. Because he cannot trust his caregiver to consistently nurture him, he shuts down his attachment system rather than live with the pain and confusion. He may become prematurely autonomous, and as a child, behave like a "little adult."

As a grown-up, he is disconnected from his emotions and body sensations. Numb to the world of feeling, he may focus on building intellectual capacity in an effort to compensate for stunted emotional and social intelligence. He avoids talking about specifics of his childhood, insisting everything was fine, though unable to recall the details. He has moved on and cannot see how his past could possibly be influencing the present.

While avoidant babies cut an emotional cord with their caregiver and repress awareness of feelings, infants raised in the Cold Café form an *anxious attachment* and have a hyperactive emotional experience. The pattern develops in response to erratic and enmeshed caregiving. Preoccupied with their own emotional material, these caregivers are unable to attune to the needs of their babies.

Rather than recognizing baby as a separate being with independent needs and interests, the caregiver intrudes and shapes baby's behavior to fit within her own window of tolerance.

Because of this conditioning the anxious child struggles to develop a healthy identity and emotional life. She may cope by expressing extreme neediness and angry resistance—and adhere to the same pattern as an adult. She struggles to see other people as unique, and when under stress, resorts to controlling behaviors to soothe her insecurities.

While avoidant and anxious infants suffer in their inner world, they generally adapt in a way that enables them to function, albeit in a numbed or neurotic fashion. Those of us with a *disorganized attachment* are not so fortunate. These are the babies raised in the Cruel Café. This baby's developing nervous system is overwhelmed by the trauma and his sense of self fragments. Growing up, his tolerance for stress is severely restricted. He may blow up or shut down when facing challenges a securely-attached peer easily shrugs off.

Research finds that nearly half the children in our society experience an early childhood akin to the Clueless, Cold or Cruel Café, developing within a continuum of confusion, conflict, insecurity, and intense igo.

THE ORIGINATOR OF ATTACHMENT THEORY, Edward John Mostyn Bowlby, was born in 1907 to a well-to-do family in London, England. His father was a renowned surgeon, and as was common for a brood of the Bowlby's station, the children were cared for by a cadre of nannies and nursemaids. John was the responsibility of a nursemaid named Minnie. The children only saw their mother for an hour each day, between 5 and 6 o'clock in the evening, and their father for visits on Sundays and holidays.

When John was four years old, he lost his surrogate mother Minnie when she left the family for a better job. At seven, he was sent away from home to boarding school. Following in his father's footsteps, John then moved on to Trinity College in Cambridge to study medicine. After three years, his interest turned to psychology. At the age of 21, he began working at a school for "maladjusted children." The experience moved him.

One of the students, a boy of sixteen, was placed at the facility after being expelled from his school for repeatedly stealing. He seemed withdrawn and emotionally distant. Bowlby learned that the boy was born in very difficult circumstances, and like his own experience, the nurse who had cared for the boy left him in early childhood.

The powerful parallel ignited a spark in the young med student. Encouraged by a supervising teacher at the school, Bowlby went on to study psychology with a focus on maternal influences on child development. While serving at London's Tavistock Clinic, Bowlby authored a pioneering paper that investigated a correlation between the deprivation of nurturing in infancy and adolescent delinquency. Soon after, the World Health Organization

(WHO) asked Bowlby to report on the psychological needs of children orphaned during the Second World War. In the report, Bowlby challenged the elite European parenting practices he experienced as a child, noting:

> What is believed to be essential for mental health is that the infant and young child should experience a warm, intimate, and continuous relationship with his mother (or mother-substitute), in which both find satisfaction and enjoyment ... each needs to feel closely identified with the other ... The services which mothers and fathers habitually render their children are so taken for granted that their magnitude is forgotten. In no other relationship do human beings place themselves so unreservedly and so continuously at the disposal of others.

To provide this constant round-the-clock attention within our own family, my wife and I decided to equally share in caregiving for our young children—from feeding and diaper changes, to late night comforting and daytime fun. Among other things, doing my fair share of the care placed me with one of our little ones in plenty of play groups, library story times, and preschool activities. On one occasion the mama discussion turned to breastfeeding—clearly not an area of deep personal expertise.

"Everyone always talks about how beautiful breastfeeding is," one mother quipped, evoking a collective groan from the sisterhood. "It can be so painful and exhausting," another sympathized. Yet, it turned out that those who were able to, chose to offer this gift to their children anyway. As Bowlby advocated, this is what makes it beautiful—wholeheartedly stepping beyond the igo to care for another despite the personal hardship—rather than an idealized image of a baby blissfully slurping from a breast.

Although breastfeeding offers a baby many benefits, including enhanced immune system functioning and IQ, research finds it is not required to create attachment security. Attachment is more about the bonds of love than the choice of breast or bottle. Simply having breast milk on the menu doesn't make life much better for a baby living in a Cruel Café. Likewise, the use of day care in and of itself is not found to weaken attachment security. Young children who are nurtured in a home like the Caring Café are empowered to spend time away from it. The strongest predictor of attachment insecurity at fifteen months of age is insensitive parenting by the infant's primary caregiver.

Some popularized approaches for "attachment parenting" imply that activities like breastfeeding, baby wearing, and co-sleeping are required to foster attachment security. However, attachment science does not seem to support this view. While such methods may be developmentally beneficial, they contribute to attachment security when they are an expression of a caregiver's sensitivity, not a substitute for it.

Paradoxically, for some caregivers, the stress of trying to perfectly practice such "attachment parenting" methods could undermine the expression of the qualities that actually enable attachment security. Said differently, the nurturing quality of the social-emotional interactions between the caregiver and infant are the essential factor in the formation of attachment security, rather than the simple satisfaction of perceived physiological needs.

In the years following the WHO report, Bowlby refined his work and went on to become the father of attachment theory. A Canadian-American colleague who joined his team for a time in London, Mary Ainsworth, became its proverbial mother. In her doctoral dissertation, written eleven years before meeting Bowlby, she had similarly concluded "where family security is lacking, the individual is handicapped by the lack of a secure base from which to work."

By secure base, Bowlby and Ainsworth were referring to the mother or other primary caregiver serving as a base of safety and security that empowers a child to courageously explore their world. Should a young child's adventure become overwhelming or painful, he is confident he can scurry back to his caregiver for protection or comfort.

Developing with the experience that his fundamental needs will be lovingly met helps a child cultivate a secure base within. A child nurtured this way may develop a sense of trust, well-being, resilience, and the capacity to regulate his emotions in the face of challenging feelings and experiences. Connected with one's basic goodness, there is less of a need to bolster the igo for protection from the pain of a seemingly hostile world.

After her time with Bowlby in London, Ainsworth conducted ethnographic field studies on mother-infant attachment in Uganda and the United States. While on the staff of Johns Hopkins University in the 1970s Ainsworth developed the Strange Situation Procedure, the experimental method that identifies an infant's attachment style.

Ainsworth's student, Mary Main, pioneered the development of the Adult Attachment Interview (AAI), a method that measures a grown-up's attachment profile. Strange Situation evaluations of infants proved to be highly-accurate predictors of psychological well-being decades down the road as measured in the AAI.

In presenting the findings of her research in Uganda, Ainsworth explained that mother-child attachment is akin to a wiring process, with the quality of their bond "built into the nervous system." In a poignant example of the power of early-childhood nurturing, research finds that combat veterans with secure attachment profiles show reduced measures of post-traumatic stress disorder (PTSD). Indeed, studies show that a soldier's attachment profile can be a stronger predictor of PTSD than the severity of the trauma they experienced in combat or as a prisoner of war.

Bowlby and Ainsworth did not intend to blame mothers or other caregivers for their shortcomings—or create even more pressure to be perfect parents. They understood that caring for young children is incredibly challenging—physically, emotionally, mentally, and financially. Most parents genuinely try to do the best they can, often with severely limited support systems. Those parents who are unable to offer the sensitive nurturing young children need generally suffer from insecure attachment issues themselves. Unconsciously, they are simply perpetuating a dysfunctional family pattern from one generation to the next.

The maternal blame game that continues in some psychology and self-help circles is counterproductive. Rather than condemning mothers or caregivers, it is wiser to help them cultivate the capacities of awareness, attunement, and empathy required to foster attachment security.

Recently, the American Academy of Pediatrics reached the same conclusion, counseling: "Health in the earliest years—beginning with the future mother's well-being before she becomes pregnant—lays the groundwork for a lifetime of physical and mental vitality ... these constitute the building blocks for a vital and sustainable society." It is an understanding many original cultures masterfully embodied for millennia.

CHAPTER 3
Original Foundations

For everything that lives is holy, life delights in life.
—*William Blake*

THE CANOPY OF A MATURE mesquite tree offers sanctuary from the scorching sun in the American Southwest. I couldn't resist a bench nestled beneath one while strolling through a park in Phoenix. Taking a seat, I savored the shade and antics of great-tailed grackles and white-winged doves bounding among the branches. Known by some original peoples of the Sonoran Desert as "the tree of life," this magnificent mesquite was teeming with it.

Before long an out-of-place object dangling from a large limb caught my eye. It looked like an enormous price tag. I squinted to decode the bold-faced text in the distance: "This tree will give $153.65 worth of environmental and aesthetic benefits over the next year." No doubt the sign was hung by a well-intentioned environmentalist. However, choosing to measure a great tree of life's value in dollars and cents unwittingly undermines the cause. How can life's intrinsic value ever be up for discussion if everything that lives is holy? When connected with our true nature, we are of the life that delights in life and willfully nurture the conditions that sustain it.

The pioneering psychologist Abraham Maslow explained the principle for human beings as an interdependent hierarchy of needs, which is often symbolized as a pyramid. The base of the structure is formed by the fulfillment of needs for our physiological survival (such as adequate air, water, food, and shelter), safety (physical and emotional), as well as the experience of belongingness, love, and esteem. Only from this secure base is further conscious development possible. Maslow concluded: "The good or healthy society would then be defined as one that permitted people's highest purposes to emerge by satisfying all their basic needs."

The importance of a secure base is well understood by architects and structural engineers, as well as developmental psychologists and neuroscientists. Il Duomo di Santa Maria Assunta, the Cathedral of St. Mary of the Assumption, offers a classic architectural example. A half-hour walk from the central train station in Pisa, Italy, tourists flock to see the Cathedral's *campanile*, better known as The Leaning Tower of Pisa.

Construction of the cathedral's ornate bell tower started in 1173. Five years later as workers added the second floor it began to sink. Built on sandy soil with a scant nine-foot foundation, the marble tower didn't stand a chance for an upright existence. It lacked a secure base.

As construction continued, masons curved the building away from the slope, hopeful the adaptation would offer a view less askew. Instead, they built a structure whose top is almost 13 feet horizontally misaligned with its bottom. Climbing the 294 steps to the roof of the sloping structure is a disorienting experience. So is growing through childhood without an original foundation of attachment security.

The developmental time frame for our stress-management systems, from 7 to 15 months of age, closely coincides with the window for mother-child attachment. Not only does the quality of nurturing affect the development of our brain and nervous system, epigenetic research finds it structurally alters our DNA.

A baby needs help from the outside for calming and soothing because the stress management capabilities of her brain are undeveloped. Over the course of thousands of attuned feedings, diaper changes, and sleep-time routines, a baby's brain and nervous system are naturally wired in a way that reflects the caring presence of her parent. Conversely, when needs are inconsistently met or interactions are disturbing, insecurity becomes a baseline experience.

Because the attachment system is so important for an infant's survival, researchers believe its functioning may have piggybacked onto our physical pain processing system. The correlation helps explain why an insecurely attached child is less likely to rebound from the physical and emotional pain of trauma or abuse—and more likely to harm her own children as a parent. According to one study, 90 percent of mothers who mistreated their children were found to be insecurely attached themselves.

Ramping up our stress system is an adaptation intended to ensure survival in dangerous circumstances. It is achieved by inhibiting frontal cortex function—the part of the brain that calms our fight-flight-freeze response. It is like someone living in an unsafe neighborhood deciding to unleash his Doberman Pinscher. Unrestrained, the dog is free to patrol the area and actively thwart an intruder. Loosening the leash of the frontal cortex has far-reaching consequences, however.

In addition to regulating our stress system and emotional surges, the frontal cortex is also the seat of executive function and our higher cognitive abilities. These functions include concentration, planning, decision making, and problem solving. The frontal cortex is also important for marshaling the will to resist temptation or overcome strong habitual responses. In short, much of what is essential for functioning as a competent, caring, creative, and responsible adult.

The weakening of these capabilities results in a way of being that is more reactive and less reflective, more impulsive than inspired, reckless rather than rational, and a propensity for addiction instead of moderation. Understanding the importance of a foundation of nurturing, many original cultures view the well-being of mothers, children, and families as a seed that must be carefully cultivated.

THE VALLEY OF OAXACA UNFOLDS in a wishbone shape beneath southern Mexico's Sierra Madre Mountains. In a shallow cave located at the tip of the valley's east fork, called Guilá Naquitz, archeologists unearthed the earliest evidence of agriculture in the Americas. While seeds of the traditional three sisters were found in the cache—corn, beans, and squash—the latter proved to be the breakthrough discovery. Seventeen such seeds were found during the excavation in 1966, a mix of gourds and squash, some wild and others cultivated. The difference was discerned by their size. Six of the seeds, identified as members of the species *cucurbita pepo,* crossed a threshold demonstrating conscious cultivation by farmers. Through radiocarbon dating performed three decades after the original archeological dig, these pepo seeds were found to be more than 10,000 years old.

Botanically, a pepo is identified as a one-celled, many-seeded berry with a hard rind. The species includes more than 800 plants, from summer and winter squashes to varieties of pumpkins and melons. Pepos offer a lesson in balance and integration with male and female flowers growing symbiotically on the same plant. When dried, pepo gourds are traditionally used to store grains or liquids and are cut to serve as utensils and bowls. They are made into rattles enjoyed by children for play and by traditional medicine practitioners for rituals of healing, purification, and protection.

Nestled under the Sierra Madre, the Valley of Oaxaca is the birthplace of Zapotec civilization. The Zapotec are known as the people of the clouds while their neighbors, the Mixtecs, are the people of the rain. And rain it does in the region, some 30 inches annually. The temperate climate and abundant moisture make the area ideal for agriculture, a kind of Mesoamerican Eden.

The Hopi mesas of Arizona are located almost 2,000 miles northwest of the Valley of Oaxaca. Anthropologists theorize the Hopi first settled in their high-desert homeland a thousand years ago, though some elders of the culture contend they have been there far longer. In either case, the Hopi mesas are the longest continually-occupied communities in the United States.

While archeologists theorize that the Hopi were once members of Mexico's ancient civilizations, Hopi oral history speaks of an initial emergence into the world from a passage within Arizona's Grand Canyon. This was followed by a great migration that led them to Mexico and other destinations in the four cardinal directions, blessing and claiming the land with symbolic stone markings still visible as petroglyphs. Mesoamerican peoples like the Zapotec are seen as fellow migrators who chose to settle down along the way rather than continue on to the ultimate destination.

At the conclusion of their journey, traditional Hopi say they returned close to where they began. There they met the Great Spirit living as a humble farmer on the mesas of northern Arizona. The Hopi migrators asked if they could settle there. The Great Spirit said they were welcome to stay if they followed a good path, living simply, caring for land and life.

With the blessings of the Great Spirit these original Hopi founded the mother village of Oraibi, which served as a cradle of their culture for millennia. The choice of location for the Hopi homeland is significant. Unlike the fertile Valley of Oaxaca, the Hopi mesas receive less than ten inches of rainfall annually.

Following the Great Spirit's guidance, traditional Hopi say they learned to cultivate corn, beans, and pepos in barren terrain without irrigation or soil enhancement. Rather than building canals or creating compost, they fully cultivated their capacities for awareness, attunement, and skillful action. Nurturing these abilities helped them recognize subtle environmental and astrological cues indicating times, places, and techniques for optimal planting and harvesting.

At a deeper level, traditional Hopi explain these qualities support them in calling upon life-sustaining energies through an intricate annual ceremonial cycle and concentrated prayer. Elders gather underground in their kivas on frigid winter days to sing to the seeds that will be planted once the soil warms. Come springtime, with planting sticks and songs of thankfulness and encouragement, prayer-fortified seedlings are lovingly placed into earth. The supportive songs continue through the harvest—as do prayers for rain and vigilant efforts to protect the budding plants from predators.

In the traditional Hopi lifeway, families are both matrilineal and matrilocal. Most property, including homes, farming plots, and ritual items are inherited through the maternal lineage. After marriage, the husband joins his wife's family. The men skillfully farm the arid land to support their families, then return the crops harvested to their wives. Once married, a man still remains a member of his birth family's own matrilineage and often returns home to assist with ceremonies and other responsibilities.

Because the vocation of nurturing home and family is honored as sacred and fundamental to the society's well-being, wealth and power are allocated accordingly. Hopi women are entrusted with the family's material wealth and share in community governance and religious duties. Just as the sanctity of the mother-child bond is at the center of traditional Hopi society, honoring both the Great Spirit and Mother Earth are central to their spiritual life.

In 1898 Elbridge Ayer Burbank, a young painter from Illinois, made an extended visit to the Hopi mesas as part of a broader cross-country journey to document American Indian culture. Living among the Hopi and other Pueblo Indians of the Southwest for many months, he found them to be hospitable, peaceful, and industrious. Indeed, of all the indigenous cultures he encountered on his journey across America, Burbank concluded, "the Hopis were the most advanced and prosperous." He observed that like other Pueblo communities, Hopi society was profoundly family-centered. He explained:

Modern psychologists say 'Be slow and gentle with children, suddenness, either mental or physical, will confuse them. Let their life fall into a routine. Let them feel they are part of the family. Let them develop as individuals and do not repress, but guide their natural interests.' This was the policy of the Indians as I observed them.

Nowhere were children more charmingly treated than among the Pueblo Indians, for example. It was rare to hear a Pueblo child cry or to hear him quarrel with his playmates. I think I never saw a Pueblo Indian strike or punish a child. And the little people were polite, gentle, and happy.

How did Indian parents accomplish this miracle? First by affection. Then, both men and women, young and old, always had time for the youngsters ... The life of the entire pueblo was slow and gentle and quiet. The bright sun rose, work in the fields and in the house went on. There was clay to play with. There were playmates and dogs and cats. Adults spoke to each other quietly, courteously. An Indian's voice is seldom raised; seldom is he inconsiderate in his speech. These habits are quickly picked up by children.

In the 1950s, then 19-year old Elizabeth Marshall Thomas moved with her family to southern Africa's Kalahari Desert to live among the Ju/wasi, considered Earth's oldest human society. Her father was fascinated by the Ju/wasi, whose ancestry can be traced back 150,000 years in the region. Although some 10,000 miles away from the Hopi mesas of Arizona, Thomas observed similar family dynamics in this "Old Way" culture:

The Ju/wasi were unfailingly good to their children. An infant would be nursed on demand and stay close to its mother, safe in the pouch of her cape, warm in cold weather, shaded in hot weather. Complete with a wad of soft grass for a diaper. Ju/wa children very rarely cried, probably because they had little to cry about. No child was ever yelled at or slapped or physically punished, and few were ever scolded. Most never heard a discouraging word until they were approaching adolescence, and even then the reprimand, if it really was a reprimand, was delivered in a soft voice. At least the tone was soft, even if the words weren't always ... The Ju/wa were every parents dream. No culture can ever have raised better, more intelligent, more likeable, and more confident children.

The notion is not to let children run wild without respect for order or authority. Instead, authority is expressed through care rather than control. Children are encouraged to learn from the natural consequences of their actions. Adults are present to redirect a young child when she approaches danger and comfort her when painful missteps inevitability occur. Rather than being told what to do, children learn through direct experience and supportive guidance.

It is no accident that original societies have lived in multigenerational family clans from time immemorial. In such extended families, many adults are present and available to help with the nurturing of young children—mothers and fathers, aunts and uncles, grandmothers and grandfathers, sisters and brothers.

As any engaged parent knows, caring for young children is an in-your-face, full-spectrum experience. If a child has special needs, the challenges are even more intense. Because young children continually vie for their mother's attention, it is incredibly difficult for her to meet her own needs and those of the larger family without help.

It never occurred to original societies to ask a mother carry this burden alone. They understood it is virtually impossible for a sleep-deprived, socially-isolated, stressed-out mother to offer the nurturing an infant needs.

When a mother in many original societies needed time to rest or renew, she knew another family member or friend was always ready to step in to care for her children once she stepped away. Modern parents dream of living with such a support system.

Christiane Northrup, MD, an international advocate for women's health and wellness, points to her own trans-formative experience of collaborative caregiving as a mother of young children:

> I remember that the best time I ever had with my children when they were little (three months and two years) was when I went to visit my mother while my sister and her children were visiting. My sister was also nursing a baby at the time, so when I wanted to go out for a while, she simply nursed Kate for me, as women have been doing for centuries. (Kate looked up at her, wide-eyed, the first time, as if to say 'Who is this?' Then she settled right down to her meal.) Our children played together happily, and I was able to enjoy the company of adults at the same time that I was enjoying my children. This was my only experience of what a loving tribe must have felt like.

The current leader of the Tibetan Buddhist Karma Kagyu lineage, the 17th Gyalwang Karmapa Ogyen Trin-ley Dorje, was born to a family of nomads in 1985 in a pristine part of the Himalayan plateau. He lived in the Tibetan Old Way until the age of seven when he left home to begin his formal Buddhist training at Tsurphu monastery. He made an arduous escape from Chinese-controlled Tibet to India as a teenager, where he now lives in exile. He made his first trip to the U.S. at the age of 23.

"I grew up in a very remote part of Tibet, far from the developed world. There were virtually no consumer goods in the entire area. Many people think of such remote places as backward," Ogyen Trinley Dorje explains. However, after experiencing the developed world, he questions such perceptions of original cultures. In his childhood he observed people generally had what they needed and were happy. There was fresh air and water and virtually no waste. Hard work was required, but family and friends had ample time to enjoy each other's company.

"In terms of satisfaction in life, might it be the developed world that is lagging behind traditional societies like the nomadic community I was born in?" Ogyen Trinley Dorje asks. "We could define development in terms of how much we are able to increase the bonds of friendship and closeness, and by how central we make community and mutual affection. When I think of a society that creates happiness, I think of a society where compassion and love replace competition and greed as the emotional forces that bind us together."

Contemporary psychological and genetic research supports this perspective. A recent study found that people with high levels of eudaimonic happiness—the sense of well-being that manifests from having a deep sense of

46

connection and meaning in life—demonstrated improved immune cell gene expression. On the other hand, people who relied on igo-based hedonic happiness associated with consumption and self-gratification showed impaired genetic expression in the same types of cells.

AT THE HEART OF INSECURE ATTACHMENT patterns are defensive strategies that feed the igo and compromise our natural capacity for compassion and cognizance. We are conditioned to retreat from the pain of connected experience into concepts. Or, we lose it in the face of intense emotional experience, blowing up, shutting down, or spacing out.

Reconnecting with compassion is aided by actively cultivating a mind full of awareness, or *mindfulness*. Such mindfulness is a way intentionally giving our attention to the fullness of the present moment without judgement or labeling. We observe the complete spectrum of feelings, thoughts, sensations, and perceptions as they arise in our field of awareness, without becoming immersed in them. Experience is met with a sense of welcoming and fresh openness that unwinds the igo's impulsive interpreting, rejecting, clinging, or altering. We learn to trust that whatever arises is okay as it is and let it be. In that space we can act kindly, wisely, and spontaneously.

Within the brain, the centering capacity of mindfulness is coordinated by the frontal cortex. As explained, this is the area of the brain that regulates our stress system and emotional surges, and processes physical and emotional pain. It is also the seat of our attachment system and higher cognitive abilities, including problem solving and impulse control. Development of the frontal cortex is often compromised in infants who experience stress and deprivation common with insecure attachment, as well as children with histories of abuse and trauma.

Likewise, research finds structural and functional deficits in the frontal cortex of individuals with antisocial, violent, and psychopathic histories. At the other end of the spectrum, brain scans of meditators proficient in the practice of mindfulness show that areas of the brain associated with attention and awareness are more highly developed.

In a groundbreaking study utilizing magnetic resonance imaging (MRI), a Harvard-affiliated research team found that participating in only 27 minutes of daily mindfulness meditation for eight-weeks caused measurable changes in brain regions associated with empathy, memory, emotional regulation, sense of self, and stress management.

Not content with the concept that mindfulness correlates with qualities that boost compassion, a university research team in the Boston area set out to test the hypothesis. Meditation classes were offered by an experienced Buddhist teacher to participants for eight weeks. The impact was compared to a group that did not receive the training through a controlled experiment.

Study participants were invited into an office waiting room with three chairs, two of which were occupied.

Upon arriving, participants naturally plopped down in the available seat. After they had been sitting for a few minutes, an actor playing the role of a "sufferer" entered the room with crutches and a leg brace, visibly wincing in pain. Those who received meditation training were five times more likely to offer their seat to the sufferer than those in the control group. In only two months the igo's influence was demonstrably debilitated, opening a connection with our heart of compassion.

While Old Way societies are sometimes considered primitive, it may be more valuable to view them as foundational. Sustainable complexity is not attained by leapfrogging over this foundation, but building upon it. Indeed, our increasingly complex and unsustainable igo-oriented societies seem more like the Leaning Tower of Pisa than an exquisite expression of human ingenuity.

Consider the Internet as an example of the principle. The complexity and richness of the content being transmitted depends completely on the integrity of the underlying infrastructure. A network built with insufficient capacity will choke when flooded with a tidal wave of video streams, tweets, and Facebook feeds. Likewise, before accelerating a race car to 200 miles per hour, the driver wants to be sure the vehicle is in top shape. A tire that wobbles at a gentle pace may become a catastrophic liability at high speeds. So it also seems is the lack of a secure base in an increasingly complex world.

As it is for a communications network, the process of optimally wiring or upgrading the infrastructure of the human nervous system is tedious and labor-intensive. Shooting, editing, and uploading a video for YouTube can be an exhilarating creative process. Operating backhoes and bucket trucks to install thousands of miles of fiber-optic cabling is comparatively grueling and glamour-free. The same is true for providing the attuned and affectionate nurturing a child requires for their optimal inner wiring. Parenting a baby with awareness, attunement, and empathy offers countless joys, but it also means many sleepless nights and exhausting days. There's not much in it for the igo.

The Hopi, Ju/wasi, and Tibetans all live in hostile landscapes. Traditionally, highly developed awareness and attunement embodied in closely-knit communities meant the difference between life and death. It is no wonder that these sensitive adults worked together to nurture aware and attuned children. Moreover, modern neuroscience suggests that the optimal integration and functioning of our awareness, attachment, and pain perception circuits may have enabled such Old Way cultures to live with an authentic sense of well-being in what we would consider to be completely inhospitable conditions.

Comparatively, it seems that many of us in technologically-developed societies are caught in a downward spiral of discomfort and disequilibrium. Insecure attachment weakens frontal cortex functioning, which undermines our sense of inner comfort and resilience in the face of physical and emotional pain. It also diminishes mindfulness and the restraint of addictive impulses.

In response, we seek ever more comfort for the igo through intoxicants, consumerism, media, apps, and sense pleasures—tools of "mass distraction" that can unwittingly aid ecological destruction. Because these escapist methods do nothing to address the root causes of the situation, the cycle of degeneration intensifies, like a snowball rolling downhill.

"Nature itself does not speak with a voice that we can easily understand. Neither can the animals and birds we are threatening with extinction talk to us. Who in this world can speak for nature and the spiritual energy that creates and flows through all life?" asked Hopi elder Thomas Banyacya. "In every continent are human beings who are like you but who have not separated themselves from the land and from nature. It is through their voice that nature can speak to us."

WITH AN INTENTION TO FOSTER a take-action approach to the ecological challenges we face, extreme athlete and adventurer Davey du Plessis set out to complete a solo 4,000-mile hike, bike, and paddle expedition. He started at the source of the Amazon River high in the Peruvian Andes with the goal of travelling the breadth of Brazil to the Atlantic Ocean. Through the journey du Plessis experienced an unexpected lesson in the power of our compassion and what can happen when we are cut off from it.

As du Plessis was paddling alongside river dolphins on a remote stretch of the Amazon, an engine-powered canoe with two men passed his kayak. Moments later du Plessis felt the piercing pain of bullets and he toppled forward into the water. After struggling to shore with remarkable determination he managed to hobble a mile in search of help. Unable to yell because of a bullet hole in his windpipe, du Plessis desperately tried to hop up and down when he saw two men of the rainforest in the distance. They brought him to their village and an entire community of original Amazonians worked tirelessly to save the life of a stranger. He recalled:

> I clearly remember an old lady taking the time and care to wash all the dried blood and mud off me with a bucket and sponge. There was another man who sang songs to me while I was being transported, and another man who prayed or chanted what felt like blessings and protection. A person, whose face I never saw, would rub my back every time I was throwing up blood. It was the small things. I must have passed through the hands of fifty individuals that night while on the way to a hospital …
>
> I survived, ultimately, because others were there to help and care for me at my time of need. When I was knocked down there had been people there to help me back up again. Despite the language and cultural barriers, all those whom I had encountered seemed to feel and understand my suffering and pain. It was beyond sympathy for my condition, it was a deep compassion and empathy that allowed the indigenous people to reach out and pool all their resources, time, and care towards ensuring the survival of a stranger.

The adventurer met fellow human beings of the life that delights in life. However, when du Plessis finally reached the nearest hospital he faced a harsh return to the world of igo where life carries a price tag. Unable to prove his identity and ability to pay, du Plessis was initially denied treatment. Thanks to a plea shared by his mother through social media, an employee of a multinational company operating in the country vouched for du Plessis and medical care was provided.

Knowing all that lives is holy we make the noble choice to cultivate an original foundation of well-being for us all.

CHAPTER 4

The Noble Heart

A noble heart lies intact within each of us …
When we clear away all that blocks it,
this heart can change the world.
—*The 17th Gyalwang Karmapa Ogyen Trinley Dorje*

RATHER THAN SITTING QUIETLY on their mats, the Buddhist monks at Namgyal Monastery in India were rolling off them in side-splitting laughter. It was not the response Richard Davidson was expecting. The American neuroscientist and a colleague had been invited by the Dalai Lama to share details about their research investigating the effects of compassion meditation on the brain.

The laughter started when Dr. Davidson's colleague placed an electrode cap on his head to demonstrate the measurement of brainwave activity. They assumed the monks were cackling because the scientist looked ridiculous in the wiring. "It turns out that they were laughing at where we were placing our electrodes," Davidson later recalled. "They thought it was hysterical that we thought the key to compassion was in the head as opposed to the heart."

The Tibetan word for compassion, *nying-je*, literally means "noble heart." Rooted in empathy, this noble heart of compassion also embodies a deep knowing of our interconnectedness, the power of reason, and a conviction to act to alleviate suffering. While we are all born with this noble heart, its expression can be impeded by our conditioning. When this happens, both spiritual and scientific traditions find we can train to awaken our noble heart's potential.

Research psychologist Phillip Shaver highlighted the link between attachment security and the capacity for compassion at a conference hosted by the Dalai Lama. Building on Bowlby and Ainsworth, Shaver and his colleagues shared that the secure base created by an attuned and responsive primary caregiver promotes a sense of connectedness and safety, as well as the ability to seek support and share it with others when needed. Their research concluded: "Attachment security provides a solid foundation for compassion and altruism, or stated the other way round, that insecurity interferes with compassion and helping."

For example, one study measured empathy toward a person who was said to have been diagnosed with cancer. Those with indications of attachment security were more compassionate than those classified as insecurely attached. Additionally, the insecurely attached subjects reported greater discomfort interacting with their ostensibly suffering peer.

The good news, Shaver and other researchers find, is that insecure attachment patterns are not written in stone. Once a sense of attachment security is fostered, empathy and compassion readily arise—at least for brief periods. In repeated experiments, psychological researchers have found that those with insecure patterns can be "primed" through conscious or subliminal techniques to feel a sense of loving connection.

When the pump is primed, compassion and empathy flow naturally. For example, mentioning words like love, hug, or close aid with priming, as do imagining feelings of safety, security, and connection. Having participants recall instances when they felt supported and loved by a caregiver also proved to be an effective primer, as did reflecting upon the compassion of religious figures such as Buddha, Jesus, Moses, Gandhi, or Mother Mary.

In a particularly powerful example, priming techniques helped weaken strong us-versus-them sentiments among the insecurely attached in Israel, a hotbed of ethnic and religious division. Once primed, participants were more willing to interact with "out-group members." For example, an Israeli Jew primed with a sense of attachment security would feel less threatened by an Israeli Arab. The researchers noted, however, that simply priming with positive feelings didn't do the trick. The cues had to specifically foster a sense of attachment security to engage empathy and compassion.

THE MOST POTENT EXPRESSION OF our noble heart is *bo-dhicitta*, the aspiration for the complete liberation of all beings. The awakening heart-mind of bodhicitta is the opposite of self-fixated igo. When we choose to cultivate bodhicitta we walk the path of the *bodhisattva,* the altruistic awakening hero.

Actively cultivating a tangible feeling of closeness, care, and concern for all living beings is an essential ingredient in awakening bodhicitta. A classic approach is visualizing all beings as having been our parents or children. The strategy is logical for cultures with a belief in reincarnation. Throughout infinite time and countless rebirths, we all would have been each other's parents and children, siblings and spouses.

The method echoes the insights of the pioneering social psychologist William McDougall who called a parent's drive to provide nurturing and protection for his or her children "the most powerful of instincts." He viewed it as "the source, not only of parental tenderness, but of all tender emotions and truly benevolent impulses … and enters in some degree into every sentiment that can properly be called love." The Dalai Lama likewise explains:

> The love and kindness shown us by our mother in this life would be difficult to repay. She endured many sleepless nights to care for us when we were helpless infants. She fed us and would have willingly sacrificed everything, including her own life, to spare ours. As we contemplate her example of devoted love, we should

consider that each and every being throughout existence has treated us this way. Each dog, cat, fish, fly, and human being has at some point in the beginningless past been our mother and shown us overwhelming love and kindness.

This recognition awakens a tangible sense of intimacy and gratitude for life. Cherishing all beings as our own parents and children naturally unleashes compassionate concern and loving-kindness. We yearn that our universal family of sentient beings find ultimate happiness and take personal responsibility to bring it about.

The method is intuitive for someone blessed with a baseline of attachment security formed with a loving caregiver. But what about those of us who are insecurely attached or experienced abuse, neglect, or trauma at the hands of a parent?

We can begin the conscious cultivation of compassion with ourselves. As we acknowledge the truth of our life's journey, compassion arises from the depths of our noble heart for the sorrow, loss, confusion, anxiety, and anger we personally carry. Honoring the truth of our actual experience then becomes the basis for authentic empathetic understanding of the plight of others. Our circle of compassion expands from ourselves to include family, friends, strangers, and even those we identify as adversaries. The genuine wish arises that we—and all beings without exception—find complete freedom from suffering.

In the bodhisattva tradition that flourished in the patriarchal societies of India and Tibet, intensive training in the cultivation of bodhicitta often occurred in a monastic context. Men and boys were encouraged to renounce earthly attachments—including their families—to focus single-mindedly on spiritual awakening. This is after all the path that Prince Siddhartha blazed on his own journey to becoming the Buddha. Overwhelmed by an initial insight into the nature of suffering, he left his wife and baby boy behind to seek a solution. After finding one he returned home to share it.

Arguably, high-minded spiritual ideals about love and compassion are most profoundly embodied in human form by parenting, nurturing, and caregiving. Rather than transcend our humanity, the essence of spiritual practice is extending our innate capacity for concern from our immediate circle to all living beings.

In his classic guidebook, *The Way of the Bodhisattva,* the Indian sage Shantideva powerfully captured the noble aspiration of the awakening hero:

> May I be a guard for those without one,
> A guide for all who journey on the road,
> May I become a boat, a raft or bridge,
> For all who wish to cross the water.
>
> May I be an isle for those desiring landfall,
> And a lamp for those who wish for light,
> May I be a bed for those who need to rest,
> And a servant for all who live in need...

Like the earth and other great elements,
And like space itself, may I remain forever,
To support the lives of boundless beings,
By providing all that they might need.

Such love is not just sweet and snuggly, but tough as nails when needed. This means actively observing and releasing our igo patterns of indifference and self-preoccupation moment by moment. Whether irritated or frustrated, overwhelmed or at our wits' end, we do our best to keep our heart open to all beings. As we inevitably fall short in upholding such an awesome aspiration, we learn to extend love, forgiveness, and understanding to ourselves too.

Whenever possible, my teacher Erma was fond of leaving the formality of the Buddhist shrine room to gather with students in the temple of natural places. When meeting in a ponderosa pine forest high upon the Colorado Plateau, she encouraged us to investigate our surroundings. "Learn from these trees. They are like great bodhisattvas," Erma explained. "They naturally breathe in what is toxic for us and selflessly breathe out what we need for survival. Can you be like them?"

As we learn to let the igo go, the felt difference between me and we loosens. We connect with our interconnectedness. Like a great tree, we come to naturally breathe in the intention "may all beings be free of suffering." Our exhalation becomes the aspiration "may all beings live in happiness," embracing and nurturing life as it is.

LIKE MANY MULTI-TASKING PARENTS, I often find myself catching up on work at coffee a shop after dropping off the kids at school or an activity. Standing in line at Starbucks one morning I noticed a "now hiring" flyer taped to the glass above the counter that read:

> *Opportunity to be more than an employee.*
> *Connect with something bigger.*
> *Have an impact every day.*
> *The opportunity is here.*
> *All you have to do is take it.*

It is easy to be cynical about marketing fluff from corporate giants like Starbucks—also known as "the mermaid store" by toddlers captivated by the logo derived from an old block-print of a twin-tailed Siren. Yes, Starbucks is tapping into human longing for transcendent purpose to drive its bottom line. However, the colossal coffee company is right in one sense. With inspired intention and action, we always have the opportunity to connect with something bigger than our igos and have an impact.

An associate at a busy Starbucks location may meet hundreds of customers a week. Rather than just serving coffee drinks, an on-the-job awakening hero may experience their activity as sharing double-shots of compassion that alleviate suffering, promote happiness, and offer a boost on the road to complete liberation. Whatever we are doing, we can always super-size the aspirations of our noble heart and act on them.

Consider the way the staff at one bustling downtown Starbucks treats a regular customer. Sally looks decades older than her actual age due to a history of hard living with mental illness and homelessness. This particular Starbucks is her daytime home. Rather than shoo her out of the store to make room for the long line of white-collar professionals stopping by on their coffee break, the staff often greets her by name. And with the help of some other customers, they have helped Sally upgrade her wardrobe.

Decked out in matching skirts, blazers, stockings, and shoes—not necessarily unruffled or deodorized—Sally orders her cup of joe and sits down at a table with an antiquated laptop computer. She turns it on and pretends to surf the web or type email to blend in with the other customers. She also mutters obscenities under her breath at the machine while the rest of us keep similar words of frustration locked behind our lips. More often than not, she is treated with tremendous dignity in the mermaid store.

In a jaw-dropping synchronicity, I once bumped into Sally twenty miles away from her usual spot. As I was waiting outside a juvenile courtroom for a foster care case hearing to begin, the door opened and out walked Sally, sobbing uncontrollably. Despite her efforts at personal improvement, I learned she was unable to clear the legal bar for recognition as a reliable caregiver. Her petition to regain custody of her children had been denied. Before long, she would no doubt be back to her one place of acceptance—Starbucks.

While the bodhicitta aspiration of complete liberation for all is audacious, it is expressed by applying awesome ideals in the messiness of everyday life. Rather than steel ourselves for spiritual battle, we are challenged to open and soften; to find the courage to be vulnerable; to risk making mistakes and fools of ourselves while giving it our best shot as awakening heroes. The opportunity is here. All we have to do is take it.

CHAPTER 5
Earned Security

Truth is within ourselves, it takes no rise
from outward things, whate'er you may believe.
There is an inner centre in us all
where truth abides in fullness.
— *Robert Browning*

WHILE HARRY POTTER GREW to become one of the most popular fictional characters on Earth, he had a rough start in life. When he was a year old, his mother and father were killed in his presence by a dark wizard. Harry too was attacked, but survived with a lightning-bolt scar etched into his forehead. Following this trauma, he was reluctantly taken in by his aunt and uncle. As they spoil their dimwitted son, they are unable to hide their resentment of Harry's presence in their home. His bedroom is a cupboard under the stairs.

Harry's awakening from this nightmare begins at the age of ten when he receives an invitation to attend the Hogwarts School of Witchcraft and Wizardry from headmaster Albus Dumbledore. Throughout Harry's years at Hogwarts, Dumbledore serves as a mentor, attachment figure, and spiritual friend as the young wizard comes to recognize and develop his latent magical abilities. Reflecting upon the character she created, author J.K. Rowling explained: "Having a child of my own reinforces my belief that children above all want security, and that's what Hogwarts offers Harry."

With nearly half of children today facing insecure attachment issues, is it any wonder Harry's story resonates so deeply with an entire generation? A child raised without a secure base, Harry finds one through Hogwarts, its headmaster, his close friends, plus his own pluck, perseverance, and mastery. It is also with Dumbledore's nurturing that the orphaned wizard comes to understand the painful story of his own life and cultivates the capacity to face its fallout.

Research finds that what happens to us in our childhood is not what determines whether we, as adults, can offer an inheritance of attachment security to our own children. Instead, a critical factor is whether our difficult childhood experiences are integrated into a coherent life narrative. Adults raised in adversity who can assimilate what happened to them are said to cultivate "earned security." Like a child born into poverty who becomes an honest millionaire, through grace and grit, those who earn their security the hard way find inner wealth and can pay it forward.

When speaking of a coherent narrative, psychologists are not referring to a well-crafted story like the adventures of Harry Potter. Instead, they are highlighting how self-compassion and awareness become the basis for coherent-ly recalling, understanding, and integrating our experience. Beyond the contents of the story, it is our ability to remain open, clear, articulate, and empathetic with challenging material that matters.

Suppressing awareness of painful experience is a use-ful short-term coping mechanism for children exposed to trauma, abuse, or neglect like young Harry. Without resources sufficiently developed to handle the situation, burying the hurt helps a child survive. The problem is the defense system continues to operate as a filter for the experience long after it is needed. What was intended to be protective instead becomes restrictive. For example, while riding a bike it is important for a kid to wear a safety helmet. However, were the helmet to become permanently affixed to his head, it would interfere with his healthy growth over the long term.

The way we are treated as children powerfully influ-ences how we treat ourselves and others. Earned security is achieved by bringing compassionate awareness to bear on these unconscious influences. Rather than trying to change what happened to us early in life, freedom is found by changing our relationship with life as it is now happen-ing. Doing so helps release patterns of the past that are conditioning our present.

An adult with lingering avoidant attachment patterns adapted as child by disconnecting from direct awareness of experience. His challenge is to learn to let go of a disproportionate reliance on the thinking mind and actively nurture awareness of feelings, body sensations, sense perceptions, and the experience of connectedness.

At the other end of the spectrum, a child with anxious attachment issues became consumed by her feelings and body sensations. Her path is about learning to remain present with the material that can be overwhelming. In either case, an insecure base that forms in early childhood is not beyond repair. Patterns of the mind and body can change; a sense of security can be cultivated and earned through self-compassion, awareness, and supportive relationships.

In the Celtic tradition of Ireland, an *anam cara* is someone who connects with us outside the igo's limitations. In Gaelic, *anam* means soul and *cara* is friend. "With the anam cara you could share your innermost self, your mind, and your heart. This friendship was an act of recognition and belonging," explains Celtic contemplative John O'Donohue. "In everyone's life there is great need for an anam cara, a soul friend, in this love you are understood as you are without mask or pretension. Where you are understood, you are at home."

While we are blessed in attuned relationships with others, we can also meet our anam cara within. When we do, we find our noble heart and inner center of truth, step out of igocentricity, and place our feet on the path toward freedom. At the heart of the journey is learning to shift from patterns of reactivity to responsiveness, from unconsciousness to awareness.

For those of us carrying the hurt of insecure attachment and other early traumas, situations are inevitably encountered that trigger these old wounds. When the pain and confusion are met with loving-kindness, clarity, and spaciousness, the patterns soften. Learning to remain present and aware with that which we have been unable to bear is an essential foundation of well-being.[*]

Loving relationships help us nurture the seed of our own basic goodness and completeness. As we come to discover this capacity within ourselves we find a psycho-emotional terra firma, a secure ground that supports us on our life's journey.

WE ARE BORN INTO A CULTURE that tells us we are somehow fundamentally flawed—from the dogma of original sin to the barrage of marketing messages claiming who we are, how we look, and what we own is not good enough. The painful feelings of inadequacy, shame, fear, and anger that come with attachment wounds and trauma unconsciously validate the argument. How could someone so defective ever be loveable? Perhaps these perceived shortcomings prevented our parents from caring for us or even made them hurt us? Maybe it was our fault.

---

[*] It is important to note that a number of evidence-based therapies, such as Eye Movement Desensitization and Reprocessing (EMDR), are found to assist with the processing and release of trauma that overwhelm our regular cognitive and neurological coping mechanisms.

While a wounded heart can't help but wonder if it is so, such feelings couldn't be further from the truth. The Tibetan word *kadak* conveys the understanding that our nature is pure from the very beginning. Our only flaw is not recognizing it and this can shift in an instant. As a child, the contemporary Tibetan Buddhist teacher Yongey Mingyur Rinpoche received an explanation about our primordial purity from his father, a renowned meditation master:

> None of our confusion and fear can change this inner purity. It doesn't get worse when we suffer or improve when we become enlightened ... We don't need to add anything to it or take anything away, nor do we have to do something to get it. It's here with us each and every moment ... The problem is that we don't recognize what we've had all along. We get so caught up in the drama of our lives that we don't see the radiant purity of our very own minds. This nature is with us even when we feel scared, lonely, and angry.

Like Harry Potter, Tibet's beloved yogi Milarepa suffered profound trauma and loss as a child, as well as abuse and neglect at the hands of his aunt and uncle. When Milarepa was seven years old, his father Sherab became seriously ill and died. On his death bed, Sherab called together his extended family asking that they promise to honor his last wishes, to which they agreed. In his will, Sherab instructed that his wealth be held in trust by his brother, who should use it to provide for Sherab's wife and children. When Milarepa was old enough to be married, he would receive the inheritance being held by his uncle.

After Sherab died, his brother and sister-in-law broke their promises and hoarded the wealth for themselves. Milarepa, his sister, and mother were beaten and worked to the bone. They were given rags for clothes and food fit for the family's animals. Through the years, Milarepa's mother Kargyen managed to secretly save enough money to pay for a party when her son reached the age of fifteen. She invited all of her extended family and announced that because Milarepa was old enough to marry and had found a fiancé, his uncle must relinquish the boy's inheritance. The uncle refused, claiming no such agreement was ever made.

Anguished over her family's plight and enraged over her brother-in-law's behavior, Kargyen again scrimped and saved. With enough in the till, she begged Milarepa to find a sorcerer who would teach him magic that could be used to punish their cruel relatives. Wishing to allay his despondent mother's suffering, Milarepa agreed.

After extensive training Milarepa succeeded in his quest. Through a series of incantations Milarepa caused a house to collapse at the wedding feast of his uncle's son, killing three dozen people. Later, Milarepa magically unleashed a massive hailstorm ruining the village's crops before harvest. While his mother rejoiced in her revenge, Milarepa was horrified by what he had done. Heartbroken, he vowed to turn his efforts to awakening his innate wisdom and compassion to help beings, rather than harm them.

Milarepa first met a meditation master who explained that his nature remained primordially pure, no matter what he had done or had been done to him. There is nothing to be acquired or attained through meditation, he counseled, as one's awakened essence is always present. "Meditate by day and become a Buddha by day. Meditate by night and become a Buddha by night. Fortunate beings whose past actions have created favorable circumstances do not even need to meditate, they are liberated by simply hearing it," the master explained.

Listening to this advice and recounting his magical abilities, Milarepa concluded he must be one of these fortunate beings. He spent his days and nights resting, rather than applying the instructions he had received. Learning of it, the master told Milarepa he was obviously confused and misunderstood the meaning of the teaching. He suggested Milarepa seek the guidance of another teacher, Marpa, a farmer and family man who had made several trips to India to study with Buddhist masters there, including the famed yogi-scholar Naropa. Hearing Marpa's name, Milarepa was filled with joy and sought out his new teacher.

Marpa had a vivid dream revealing that a young man who would become his foremost student would soon be arriving. However, once they met, Marpa put Milarepa through a series of trying ordeals, including building and dismantling four huge stone towers, and berated him whenever he asked for spiritual instruction. It was a harsh igo-eradication regimen.

In the end, Marpa introduced Milarepa to the true nature of his own mind and explained the hardships were necessary to purify the tremendous suffering he had caused through his misuse of magic. He instructed Milarepa to intensively meditate alone in mountain caves, which Milarepa did, wearing only a thin cotton robe during the freezing Himalayan winters. Through his perseverance, Milarepa fully recognized his awakened nature and taught many disciples to do the same through spontaneous songs of realization. He became renowned as one of Tibet's greatest masters of awareness.

Our innately pure essence is said to be like a diamond: indestructible, clear, and radiant. Even if it is buried in mud and obscured from plain view, our diamond-like nature is still present and its qualities remain unchanged. The traumas Milarepa experienced as a child, and the immense pain he caused by avenging them, never diminished his own innate purity. It simply buried his awakening seed deeper underground. More work was required to cultivate it, but he did so with tremendous passion and determination.

When Milarepa's own devoted student, Gampopa, was ready to leave his master, Milarepa offered to share his most precious spiritual instruction. After making Gampopa promise that he would cherish the teaching and put it to use, Milarepa bent over and lifted the back of his robe. The student saw his teacher's buttocks were thickly calloused from years of meditation on the stone floors of frigid alpine caves.

"There is no more profound teaching than this. Now you can imagine the hardships I have undergone. My attainment of great realization came from this," Milarepa said. "This is the essence of my teaching. Whether you become a Buddha or not depends on effort. With it, there can be no question about your liberation."

UNDERSTANDING AND INTEGRATING our life story supports our awakening journey. And yet, any story is just that—a collection of memories, concepts, and labels about our experience. No matter how clear and cohesive the story, our inner interpreter is still narrating a personal memoir.

The Buddhist tradition explains the nature of mind, memories, thoughts, and feelings to be empty of intrinsic existence. Unquestioningly accepting such mind contents as real, we allow ourselves to be conditioned by them. The point is not to sweep our thoughts and feelings under the rug by simply labeling them as illusory, but to experience them fully while genuinely realizing their insubstantiality.

Breaking through the igo's clouds of conceptual and emotional confusion into the presence of clear, unconfined openness has long been the experience of mystics and meditators. For some, the experience of wide-open awareness beyond conceptuality is the natural fruition of many years of sustained spiritual practice, a gradual and systematic erosion of conditioning. For others, it is an unexpected breakthrough that shatters preconceptions and leaves a gaping hole in the story we thought we knew about ourselves.

It is not merely the absence of thought or the solid sense of an igoic self that is liberating, but the spontaneous presence of awareness of our mind's empty, spacious, and loving nature. This recognition is a fundamental frame shift from identifying with the contents of the mind to understanding them to be part of a conditioned process. Any thought, feeling, or sensation which arises may be experienced merely as an expression of our mind's innate empty purity, like a wave forming, cresting, and dissolving back into the ocean. From this recognition, genuine love and compassion naturally arise for all beings suffering from a disconnection with the truth of who we are.

William James earned his doctor of medicine from Harvard Medical School in 1869 but never practiced. Instead, he served as a professor at Harvard for more than 30 years, first teaching physiology and anatomy, and later philosophy and psychology. Finding relief from his own suffering through spiritual inquiry, he extensively studied the accounts of mystics and contemplatives. During a series of lectures in 1902 he offered insights into *The Varieties of Religious Experience.*

Speaking of transformative spiritual awakenings, James concluded: "The only thing that it unequivocally testifies to is that we can experience union with something larger than ourselves and in that union find our greatest peace." Through his research James found that this opening "so often comes about, not by doing, but by simply relaxing and throwing the burden down."

James concluded that those who experienced an authentic spiritual transformation lived through a state of assurance, rather than belief. The Swiss psychologist Carl Jung referred to this recognition of deep coherence, wholeness, and unity as discovering the Self. He counseled that the journey is unique for everyone. While we may gain inspiration from psychological or spiritual superheroes, merely mimicking their path may inhibit us from discovering our own. No one steps into the same river twice.

CHAPTER 6
Know with the Flow

Flow with whatever may happen
and let your mind be free.
— *Chuang Tzu*

MOST OF ASIA'S GREAT rivers begin high in the Himalayas
of Tibet, the Land of Snow and rooftop of the world. The
Yangtze River is the continent's longest, flowing nearly
4,000 miles across China to Shanghai and the sea. The
Yarlung Tsangpo River begins southeast of Mount
Kailash in western Tibet. It flows eastward through the
Tsangpo Gorge and becomes India's Bramhaputra River,
eventually meeting the great Ganges. The Ganges River
itself begins in the Indian state of Uttarakhand, flowing
from the Himalayas through India into Bangladesh and
the Bay of Bengal.

The Mekong River originates in eastern Tibet, flowing 3,000 miles south through China, Burma, Laos,
Thailand, Cambodia, and Vietnam. The Indus River is
born near Lake Mansarovar in Tibet, meandering 2,000
miles through Ladakh, Kashmir, and Pakistan to the

Arabian Sea. The Irrawaddy, Salween, Sutlej, and Yellow Rivers also begin on the Tibetan Plateau. Together, the headwaters of the Himalayas are the source of rivers supporting some 4 billion people in eighteen Asian countries—half of Earth's human population.

In philosophy, psychology, and spiritual traditions, rivers and streams are a common metaphor for the flow of our lives, our minds, and universal forces. The Scottish philosopher Alexander Bain introduced "stream of consciousness" into the Western lexicon. His contemporary William James similarly commented on mind's activity: "It is nothing jointed; it flows. A 'river' or a 'stream' are the metaphors by which it is most naturally described. In talking of it hereafter, let us call it the stream of thought, of consciousness, or of subjective life."

In the Buddhist tradition, the ancient Indian phrase *citta-samtana* literally means "the stream of mind." Tibetans translated the term as *sem gyud*. This stream refers to the flow of one's consciousness through limitless space and time, taking birth, experiencing a life of pleasure and pain, dying, and repeating the cycle. The true nature of mind is recognized as pure awareness, or *rigpa* in Tibetan. This subtle awareness is unborn, unending, unchanging, and beyond suffering. Through meditation training the practitioner learns to differentiate between subtle unborn awareness and the coarser thoughtstream of our conventional igoic conditioning. As one more deeply connects with the former, conditioned patterns of the latter naturally melt away.

The Bengali Buddhist master Tilopa, forefather of the Mahamudra meditation tradition Milarepa later expanded in Tibet, lived as a wandering yogi in India. The prefix of his name "tilo" is the word for sesame seed in his native language. He earned it through one of his day jobs, grinding sesame seeds to release and capture their oil. Tilopa taught that his trade offered the perfect metaphor for the awakening path. Like sesame oil concealed within a seed, our already-present enlightened essence may be released under supportive conditions. Along the banks of the Ganges, he explained the development of meditative experience to his student Naropa:

> In the beginning mind is like a turbulent river. In the middle it is like the River Ganges, flowing slowly. In the end it is like the confluence of all rivers, like the meeting of mother and son.

To cultivate meditative realization, Tilopa advised Naropa not to recall, imagine, think, examine, or control thoughts and feelings. Instead he was instructed to rest his awareness naturally with whatever arrises—let go of what has passed, what may come, and what is happening. "Relax, right now, and rest." Instead of micromanaging the contents of the mind, simply become aware of and remain present with its natural flow.

Two of China's great mystics, Lao Tzu and Chuang Tzu, lived beside the Yangtze River. Through the practice of letting things be as they are, they explained one recognizes *tao*—the way that is in harmony with universal natural flow. In his *Tao Te Ching,* Lao Tzu describes tao as the infinite, unchanging, eternally present, mother of the universe that "flows through all things, inside and outside, and returns to the origin of all things."

Without recognition of unborn awareness—and when left to its own devices—the igo separates and divides unity, overlaying natural flow with its filters. Theistically speaking, such an orientation rejects reverence for divine creation in favor of human invention. Seeing the situation clearly, Israel's King Solomon warned in the Old Testament: "There is a way which seems right to a man, but its end is the way of death."

As IT CONTAINS THE MOST snow and ice on Earth after the North and South Poles, the Tibetan Plateau is known as the Third Pole. Over the past fifty years, more than 80 percent of the region's glaciers have retreated. During the same period, temperatures on the Tibetan plateau have increased at a pace three times faster than the average warming rate for the planet as a whole. If current trends continue, two-thirds of the plateau's glaciers could be gone by mid-century.

Himalayan glacial melting is exacerbated by concentrations of "black carbon" released by neighbors in the region. A primary cause is the use of biofuels for cooking, such as wood and dung, by Southeast Asia's immense population. The brown clouds created by black carbon emissions dramatically increase solar heating of the atmosphere. Continuing changes to the glaciers that source the Himalayan headwaters of Asia's great rivers could mean great hardships for the half of humanity that depend on them downstream.

In an effort to hedge its bets against cycles of floods and droughts—and to ensure a water supply for itself—China has embarked upon a massive dam-building project, including many on the Tibetan plateau. Blocking the natural flow of the Himalayan watershed is a dismaying development for Tibetans who preserved and protected the environment for millenia. The Buddha taught that *dharma* is universal truth and natural flow—akin to the *tao*—while *samsara* is the suffering that results when one is ignorantly diverted from it.

Not only are the natural flows of China's rivers being interrupted, the water itself is becoming progressively toxic due to industrial and agricultural pollution. While every society marches toward rapid industrialization with ecological damage, China's explosive growth offers an extreme example of the actions threatening life on Earth. Is there another way?

"There *is* another way, if you have the courage. The first I could describe in familiar terms because you have seen it, as we all have seen it, illustrated, more or less, in lives of those about us. The second is unknown, and so requires faith—the kind of faith that issues from despair. The destination cannot be described; you will know very little until you get there; you will journey blind. But the way leads towards possession of what you have sought for in the wrong place ... Both ways are necessary. It is also necessary to make a choice between them." — T.S. Eliot, *The Cocktail Party*

MASTERS OF AWARENESS UNDERSTAND the importance of nurturing natural flow. Following it was the way they not only survived, but thrived, in the harshest of conditions. Whether the words are from Lao Tzu, Solomon, the Buddha, or indigenous wisdom keepers, the conclusion of the sages is that, ultimately, there are only two ways of life—one that is aware, attuned, loving, and in harmony with natural flow, and one that is not. It is a binary proposition.

Original societies flowed with natural cycles rather than conceptualized clock time, relying upon awareness of sunrise and sunset, the heavenly constellations and earthly seasons. They were informed by blossoming wildflowers and falling leaves, the migrations of birds and butterflies, hibernating bears and snakes, the moon's waxing and waning, the day's warmth and the night's chill, their own breath and heartbeat, and a baby's cry for food or comfort.

As mothers, women are the headwaters of humanity. Like glacial melting, once a mother's water breaks, her baby will soon flow through her birth canal and into the human sea. When a mother is supported in providing loving and attuned nurturing, her baby may form a secure attachment. The child may naturally develop a sense of trust and connectedness, awareness and attunement, confidence and compassion, providing a secure base for a balanced human being, family, and society.

In the rush toward progress, our world has abandoned its original foundation. We are now born into a culture that is deeply disconnected from natural flow. As a baby must attach to even an unreliable caregiver for survial—albeit insecurely—we bond to the imbalanced societal patterns which welcome us at birth. With clarity, as T.S. Eliot observed, we may come to notice the degenerate and disharmonious way of the igo-driven world about us. Our despair about the predicament may bring forth a desire to regain another way of being. We understand that while both ways—alignment and misalignment with natural flow—exist in the polarities of earthly existence, it is up to each one of us to make a choice between them.

ORIGINALLY A NAUTICAL PHRASE, "Outward Bound" refers to the moment a ship departs on a new voyage. It eventually became the name of a school in Britain founded to help young sailors cultivate the courage and confidence needed to flourish in challenging conditions on the open seas. Outward Bound later became an international organization helping individuals develop these capacities through wilderness training.

The backcountry journey places a motivated learner into a challenging environment to induce a state of "adaptive dissonance." That is, a stressful experience which requires problem-solving and cooperation to regain equilibrium. The competence developed in response to the tests is empowering and offers a frame shift for the participant, reorienting them toward an engaged mode of living and learning. As the journey deepens, a solo excursion in the wilderness further strengthens self-reliance and confidence.

Our lives may seem like a spiritual outward bound experience. Dropped off in the boondocks of igoic imbalance—a family and society far removed from natural flow—we are challenged to find our way home and help others do the same. The farther from this flow we find ourselves, the greater our suffering and urgency to correct course.

"Go with the flow" has become a modern mantra for stress management. But what if the flow is a never-ending merry-go-round, or worse yet, a conveyor belt heading toward a wood chipper? Stepping off the ride would be a far better choice than circling endlessly or passively drifting toward doom. And yet, rather than question the fitness of the flow we find ourselves in, the common approach is to adapt to it in a myriad of ways. It is not unlike buying earplugs to dampen the noise of an incessant car alarm rather than figuring out how to shut it off.

For example, there has been a twentyfold increase in the consumption of medications for attention deficit hyperactivity disorder (ADHD) over the past three decades. Research psychologist Alan Sroufe notes that three million American children are currently prescribed ADHD drugs to improve their ability to concentrate. While improvements may occur in the short-term, evidence of consistent long-term academic and behavioral benefits from ADHD medications is elusive.

"The large-scale medication of children feeds into a societal view that all of life's problems can be solved with a pill," Sroufe advocates. "The illusion that children's behavior problems can be cured with drugs prevents us as a society from seeking the more complex solutions that will be necessary. Drugs get everyone—politicians, scientists, teachers, and parents—off the hook."

Sroufe, and other like-minded professionals, are not suggesting that pharmaceuticals are always a flawed treatment approach for behavioral and mental health issues. Doctors find medications can make a positive difference in the lives of many patients. That said, the explosion in diagnoses and prescription treatments for conditions like ADHD point to deeper structural issues. Besides broadly medicating children, are we not compelled to adjust ways of life that require such solutions in the first place?

On so many issues of importance, as individuals and societies, we have become hooked on being let off the hook. For the igo, it is simply too painful to consider Solomon's warning that our way which seems so right, may actually be a way that is also destructive. In the language of Alcoholics Anonymous, creating excuses to avoid changing damaging habits is colorfully called "stinking thinking."

"How is it that people can so blatantly contradict themselves, yet not be able to recognize it even if it is pointed out?" asks Abraham J. Twerski, MD, a psychiatrist, Rabbi and director of an addiction recovery center. "In one word, the answer is denial. Much of the denial in addictive, distorted thinking is due to intense resistance to change. As long as someone denies reality, he or she can continue behaving the same as before. Acceptance of reality might commit him or her to the very difficult process of change."

The answer is not simply for us to dismantle our complex technological societies, condemn pharmaceuticals, or naïvely try to return to pre-industrial simplicity. Rather, we are all called to break through the grip of igo; to cultivate the capacities of awareness, attunement, and empathy that have collectively atrophied; to reconnect with the flow that naturally knows how and where to go, just as a melting mountain glacier naturally becomes a mighty river running to the sea.

> *What the caterpillar calls the end of the world,*
> *the master calls a butterfly.*
> — *Richard Bach*

THE DENSE CANOPIES OF ENORMOUS silk cotton trees in Guatemala's Tikal National Park tower over the ruins of an ancient abandoned Mayan city. A thousand years ago Tikal's original residents wove fibers from such trees into lightweight clothing, providing a cool covering in the hot jungle.

"Anthropologists say the Maya disappeared from this land, but as you can see, we are still here," noted Don

Alejandro Cirilo Perez Oxlaj, a thirteenth-generation Quiche Maya priest and leader of the country's National Maya Council of Elders. He was speaking with a small group of visitors on a steamy spring day in 2006 before offering a fire ceremony beside an immense stone pyramid built by his people long ago.

"The indigenous people think not only for today, but for our children, their children and future generations. We all live from the same sun, earth, and water," Alejandro advised. "People are gathering large amounts of money, but it will be worthless if we destroy the atmosphere. Let's try to preserve the beauty of Mother Earth. We are all flowers of the earth, different colors and scents. We sing different songs, but they are all to the same Creator. Love each other. The earth is for all, the water is for all. These are the messages of my ancestors. Take them with you. Talk about them."

Don Alejandro's heartfelt words were born from hard-earned experience. Almost eighty years old and standing less than five feet tall, his springy legs still propelled him to the top of a giant pyramid at a pace of men half his age. Like many Guatemalan youngsters unable to afford school, he worked the streets as a shoeshine boy to help put food on his family's table. A good-natured attorney who was a regular customer taught him how to read and write during spit-and-polish sessions. Beyond extreme poverty, Alejandro survived a 36-year genocidal civil war that ravaged the Mayan highlands. His gentleness and kindness offered a remarkable contrast to the violence that decimated his homeland.

Acutely aware of the hype and hysteria twisting traditional teachings of the Maya into an apocalyptic prediction for the end of the world in the year 2012, Alejandro was eager to help set the record straight. With his wife and translator, he explained that Mayan day keepers use several calendars, including the "long count," that measures a 5,125-year cycle of the sun. In his tradition, Alejandro shared, it is understood that humanity is nearing the end of the fourth measured cycle. "This is not the end of the world, this is the end of a period of the sun," he clarified. "Now is the fourth world, next will be the fifth."

He believed the misunderstandings related to prophecies carried by Mayan spiritual elders about the "year zero," the transition time between the fourth and fifth cycles. While the prophecies warn of catastrophes that could result from people failing to care for each other and our environment, Alejandro noted that the exact timing of the year zero is actually unclear.

"The Mayan and Gregorian calendars do not coincide. Five hundred years ago during the invasion, they killed our elders, the carriers of wisdom, and burned our books. With all that missing, we're not sure about the 2012 date," he explained. "The year zero could be in 2015 or even 2020. In any case, don't fear. Continue with faith and love for the Creator and Mother Earth. You with faith may be able to see what is happening. Nothing will happen to you. You will be witnesses."

For those doubting the risks of our present trajectory, Alejandro offered simple advice: cultivate awareness of our actual situation. "Contemplate nature. Look at the mountains, the rivers, the lakes. What used to be a river is dry. What was a forest is a desert. The lakes are drying out slowly. The air we breathe is contaminated. The predictions the ancestors left in stone are coming true."

Even so, Alejandro was not preaching prophetic doom and gloom. "For the Maya, this is not a time of fear, but a period of joy," he shared. "All periods of time end. Soon, we will be able to walk like the rivers and fly like the birds, with no boundaries. It is the laws of men that have divided us, but that will come to an end. When that happens, let's welcome it. Be a messenger of these words you hear."

CHAPTER 7
The Net Effect

There was a turtle by the name of Bert and
Bert the turtle was very alert; when danger
threatened him he never got hurt
he knew just what to do.
—*Duck and Cover*

A GENERATION OF AMERICAN CHILDREN learned that during a nuclear attack safety could be found by hiding under their school desks and curling into a fetal position. The kid-friendly character Bert the turtle showed them how in the U.S. Federal Civil Defense Administration instructional film *Duck and Cover,* released in 1952. Two-and-a-half years earlier the Soviet Union detonated its first nuclear weapon, joining America in the ranks of the atomic elite and ushering in a Cold War that would continue for more than 40 years.

While children were hiding under their desks, Paul Baran was busy working at his. An engineer at the RAND Corporation, Baran was developing ideas for a "survivable" communications network—one which could continue to operate following a nuclear strike. At the time most communications networks, including AT&T's Bell telephone system, required a persistent connection between two points to operate. If either end point or elements of the connection between them were impaired, communication would be impossible. Without continuing contact among government leaders, the military, and civil defense teams, crisis could cascade into chaos.

Thinking outside the box of the telephone and radio systems of his day, Baran concluded that data communications through a distributed computer network would prove the most resilient solution in the event of an atomic attack. For many of his contemporaries, the notion was difficult to grasp. They were accustomed to an approach that better resembled tin cans connected by string.

Baran refused to give in to the static and encouraged others to persevere as well. "It would be treacherously easy for the casual reader to dismiss the entire concept as impractically complicated," Baran counseled leaders of the United States Air Force in a classified memorandum. "The temptation to throw up one's hands and decide that it is all 'too complicated' ... should be deferred until the fine print is read." Kindred scientists and engineers ultimately embraced the concept, as did the U.S. military.

J. C. R. Licklider, a psychologist and computer scientist, proposed the creation of a distributed data communications network before Baran did. However, Baran offered a nuts-and-bolts approach to help bring the seed Licklider planted to fruition. In an April 1963 memo outlining the agenda for a meeting in Palo Alto, Calif. to discuss his interconnected idea, Licklider explained the concept was founded upon "things that I feel intuitively, not things that I perceive in clear structure." He hoped that open collaboration with peers would help realize his vision more rapidly. A key issue to be addressed, Licklider concluded, was how to help incompatible computer systems learn to share with each other. He explained: "The problem is essentially the one discussed by science fiction writers: how do you get communications started among totally uncorrelated 'sapient' beings?"

In October of that year, Licklider was appointed to lead a unit at the U.S. Defense Department's Advanced Research Projects Agency (ARPA). In 1967, ARPA started building a network using Baran's architecture that would ultimately help realize Licklider's vision. The first four nodes of the so-called ARPAnet became operational in early 1970.

By 1981, the ARPAnet had grown to about 200 computers and developed the basic suite of protocols for the Internet we know today. By 1990, the emerging Internet had grown to more than 150,000 computers and was expanding rapidly. Around that time, Tim Berners-Lee, a computer scientist working at the CERN high-energy physics lab in Switzerland, contributed two missing threads to the emerging network fabric—hypertext transport protocol (HTTP) and hypertext markup language (HTML)—the enabling code for the World Wide Web. The rest is history.

The reach of the Internet—an interconnected network of networks—is astounding by contemporary measures. More than 3 billion people use the web and social media. Information is available through more than 60 trillion web pages and over a 200 billion emails are sent each day. As impressive as the Internet is, it pales in comparison to the networks that conceived it—the human brain and nervous system behind our mind.

The human brain contains some 200 billion cells, called neurons. Within our skulls we have as many neurons as there are stars in the Milky Way galaxy that is Earth's home. Each neuron may form 10,000 or more links with other neurons, creating a network with more than 200 trillion connections—more than the number of stars in our known universe. These connections are made electrically and chemically in synapses, the space between neurons. Energy and information collected through the central nervous system flows through these synapses and is processed by neurons with highly specialized functions.

Because neurons integrate as they cooperate, it is said that those that fire together wire together. As the same task is performed repeatedly by a group of neurons, a pathway is built among them. The more the pathway is used, the stronger the connection becomes until eventually a circuit is created within the brain. These neural pathways are essential enablers for our memory, perception, cognition, and action.

These pathways operate through the synchronization of neural firing patterns. The energy flows pulsate in coherent rhythms. Attuned and integrated patterns are representative of a balanced and healthy brain. Irregular rhythms, by comparison, are associated with illnesses such as schizophrenia. The implication is that these, and other conditions, are related to the way brain cells communicate and integrate. Neurons which are out of synch fail to link, undermining functioning.

While attachment pioneer John Bowlby was developing his initial theories on bonding between mother and child, Canadian psychologist Donald Hebb proposed a bonding process for neurons. "The general idea is an old one, that any two cells or systems of cells that are repeatedly active at the same time will tend to become 'associated', so that activity in one facilitates activity in the other," Hebb noted. In other words, their attunement yields a functional bond to optimize collaboration. Since then, researchers have come to understand that mother-baby bonding profoundly affects neuronal and synaptic development.

Most of our neurons are present at birth, but only a fraction of possible synaptic connections among them have been made. Many of these critical neural connections are formed during early childhood. "Repeated, multiple failures by a caretaker to attune, much research suggests, can have lasting effects," notes *Social Intelligence* author Daniel Goleman. He explains:

> When reprised throughout childhood, these patterns shape the social brain in ways that make one child grow up delighted with the world, affectionate, and comforta-

ble with people, while others grow up sad and with-drawn, or angry and confrontational. Once, such differences might have been attributed to the child's 'temperament,' a stand-in for genes. Now the scientific action centers on how a child's genes may be set by the thousands of routine interactions a child experiences growing up.

The conduit for the flow of energy and information through a neuron is its axon. The speed of the flow depends on how much myelin coats it. A fatty sheathing, myelin acts as an insulator. The more myelin, the more energy the axon may process, increasing conduction velocity for the neuron. An axon with limited myelin may deliver data as slowly as an old copper telephone line, while a myelin-rich axon acts like a super-fast fiber-optic Internet connection. Brain researchers have found that nerve impulses can zoom through axons 100 times faster when they are thickly coated with myelin.

The development of myelin is a gradual process, starting in the womb and continuing through the months following birth. The rate and extent of myelination is affected by early experience, in addition to genetic blue-prints. Although most myelin-coated pathways are laid down in the early years, for some areas of the brain, such as the frontal cortex, myelination continues into early adulthood.

The ability of the brain to change, either toward beneficial integration or dysfunctional fragmentation, is known as neuroplasticity. Thanks to the brain's neuroplasticity—its ability to rewire—weak connections can be enhanced and new ones created throughout our lifespan. The Buddha taught his students "with our thoughts we create the world." Neuroscientists clarify that our thoughts and experiences help shape the structure of our brains, through which our worldview is created.

A team at Emory University developed a secular therapeutic modality called Cognitively-Based Compassion Therapy (CBCT) derived from the Buddhist mind-training tradition embodied by modern teachers like His Holiness the Dalai Lama. After first teaching it to adults, CBCT was later tested in a controlled study with teenagers in Georgia's foster care system, a population of children disproportionately exposed to trauma, loss, physical and sexual abuse, and insecure attachment challenges.

The study found that those teens participating in six weeks of CBCT training reported reduced anxiety and increased feelings of hopefulness. Those teens practicing CBCT the most showed the greatest improvements in these measures. Additionally, through saliva tests, researchers noted the teens engaging in CBCT showed reductions in C-reactive protein, a key inflammatory marker.

Researchers were encouraged because many chronic illnesses, including cardiovascular disease, type 2 diabetes, dementia, cancer, and depression are correlated with physical inflammation exacerbated by stress and trauma. The research showed that transforming our relationship

with thought and feeling patterns translated into physiological changes affecting the body and brain.

IN A REMARKABLY SHORT time span by historical stand-
ards, the Internet has become deeply embedded in the
fabric of our lives. Through the Net we can now find
information on any conceivable subject, purchase almost
any product for delivery, earn a living, invest in the stock
market, download a library full of books, music, and
movies, and share what's going on through social media.
Enamored with its wonders, it is easy to forget the Internet
developed in response to a critical question: How can we
connect and respond in a time of crisis when the conventional ways of doing so would fail?

Humanity continues to grapple with this question.
Although the Cold War ended more than two decades ago,
we still face grave challenges to life on Earth. Taking Bert
the turtle's advice to duck, cover, and hide within our
shells won't improve the situation. We're better off heed-
ing the counsel of Internet pioneers Licklider and Baron.
They noted, respectively, that our critical challenge is
connecting with others who seem "totally uncorrelated,"
and when faced with this daunting task, resist the temptation to throw up one's hands and decide that it is all too
complicated.

Rather than some homogenous collection of computers designed from the ground up by meticulous engineers,
the Internet is an unruly hodgepodge of networks, devices,
applications, and the people who use them. Its reach grew

organically, rather than by central planning, as more people and gadgets learned how to connect. A miracle of the Internet is that any device or person can connect without fundamentally changing what or who they are. An iPhone doesn't need to morph into a Windows computer to exchange email, nor must Skype software transform into a telephone to call one a thousand miles away.

Even so, the personalization algorithms of Internet search engines, news feeds, and social networks can unwittingly divide us too. Social activist Eli Pariser noticed that contrary points of view were being edited out of his search results and social media feeds. The personalization algorithms of these services tracked what he viewed most and gave him more of what he seemed to like, cutting out opportunities to be exposed to alternate perspectives.

Over time Pariser felt as if he were becoming trapped in a "filter bubble." Instead of connecting us with a range of people and viewpoints, a hyper-personalized Internet can leave us "isolated in a web of one." So does a predominately conceptual or emotionally-reactive orientation. Devoid of empathetic connections, social bonds may instead be formed on the basis of shared igo-based filter bubbles. Only those with matching views are allowed into the circle. Anyone with different ideas or values becomes a strongly separate other, an enemy "them" that is irreconcilably different from "us."

This filtering tendency was documented in a study investigating the way we integrate views from scientific experts on issues posing great societal risks, such as climate change and gun control. The experiments found that people better remember expert opinions that fit their preconceptions. Now called confirmation bias, Sir Francis Bacon observed the pattern in play four centuries ago, noting it "draws all things else to support and agree with it …[so] the authority of its former conclusions may remain inviolate."

Without a willingness to step out of locked-in conceptual or feeling loops, the gap between filter bubbles may never be bridged. It is easy to spot this pattern playing out in the polarization fueled by hyper-partisan politics and media.

David Bohm was among the most accomplished theoretical physicists of the 20th century. Over time his inquiries expanded from quantum mechanics to exploring the mechanics of human suffering and ecological degradation. The hidden culprit, Bohm concluded, is the unbridled influence of our igoic interpreter that clings to its thoughts about how things are.

Once the igo interpreter or emotional reactor is chosen over empathetic awareness, our direct connection with the natural world and our divinity and is impeded. This could be considered a kind of original sin, at least in the sense of the Greek word for it, *hamartia*. It means "to miss the mark," such as an error in aim that causes an archer's arrow to sail past its target. Wishing for happiness, we aim for it, but instead find ourselves stuck in cycles of suffering we unconsciously perpetuate.

Both religious fundamentalism and rigid atheism are igo-driven feedback loops. Scriptural literalists of any religion recycle representations of divinity as dogma, rather than experience living truth in the present. The infinite is divided up into manageable bits, locked into a box for safe keeping, and defended to the end. With religious fundamentalism there is no openness to a new view; indeed, the proclivity is to actively deny such possibilities—a hallmark of igo. What is supposed to be a catalyst for compassion and altruism instead becomes a driver of division and animosity. In the words of psychologist John Welwood, annexing divinity to perpetuate self-centered patterns amounts to taking a "spiritual bypass" on the awakening journey.

PETER SENGE AND OTTO SCHARMER serve on the faculty of the Sloan School of Management at the Massachusetts Institute of Technology (MIT). Together with consultants Joseph Jaworski and Betty Sue Flowers, they observed patterns of separation stifling the capacity for creativity, caring, and change in organizations around the globe. They found that the key to becoming free from these patterns is the capacity to "suspend." The process involves removing ourselves from the habitual stream of the igo's assumptions and reactions. Doing so, however, requires courage and clarity.

"When we truly suspend taken-for-granted ways of seeing the world, what we start to see can be disorienting and disturbing, and strong emotions like fear and anger arise, which are hard to separate from what we see. To the extent we're trying to avoid these emotions, we'll avoid suspending. To the extent we can't talk about any of this, it limits all of us," Senge explains.

Senge and his colleagues note that the process of suspending at first feels unsettling. Thus, the personal work required of each of us to authentically connect is developing the ability to remain aware and present with our thoughts and emotions—rather than suppressing or being swept away by them. "A virtually infinite variety of meditative and contemplative methods from Western, Eastern and native traditions are available to help build our capacity to slow down and gradually become aware of our 'thought stream.' What matters most is not the particular method we choose but our willingness to make our own cultivation a central aspect of our life," they counsel.

My teacher Erma delighted in challenging students to suspend their fixed ideas about spirituality. To kick start the process, Erma would give students research assignments and encourage them to report on their findings to the community. Like an inflated balloon, once a student's concepts had sufficiently expanded they were easier to pop. My bubbles were burst repeatedly. On one occasion another student was asked to report on the Buddhist path. He selected a classic text outlining twelve aspirations for awakening. The first seven aspirations were shared in sequence, followed by the eighth, which reads:

> I vow that in a future life when I attain awakening, if
> there are women who give rise to a deep loathing for
> their female body and wish to renounce it because they
> are oppressed and disturbed by the myriad sufferings of
> being female, upon hearing my name, they will be able
> to turn from women into men who are replete with male
> features and ultimately realize unsurpassed awakening.

"Stop right there," Erma barked. "That is among the craziest things I have heard." Serious Buddhists in the room gasped as a line from the scriptural cannon was questioned. Long-time students who knew Erma's proclivities politely swallowed their laughter.

"Of course being a woman can be your spiritual path," Erma continued. "To awaken, you never need to be someone other than who you are."

There are many colorful examples in the Buddhist tradition of spiritual practitioners having their concepts suspended—and sometimes eviscerated—by cantankerous women known as wisdom *dakinis*. One of the most famous of those stories involves the scholar-turned-yogi Naropa, the teacher of Marpa, Milarepa's master.

Naropa was an accomplished scholar at Nalanda University, India's preeminent Buddhist institution in his day with some 10,000 monastic students. Because of his academic prowess, Naropa was appointed guardian of Nalanda's north gate, essentially placing him in the role of a philosophical bouncer. In that era, the proponent of any spiritual discipline could knock on one of the university's gates and demand a debate to the finish. The loser of the intellectual duel was required to renounce their philosophical system and become a disciple of the victor.

One day Naropa was holding office hours within the academy, reading from a collection of Buddhist scriptures, when an old woman interrupted him. "That text you are reading, is it the words you understand or do you understand the meaning?" she asked.

"It is the words I understand," Naropa replied. The woman was overjoyed with his response and jubilantly started singing and dancing. As she carried on, Naropa thought that if she became this happy hearing he knew the words, she would be ecstatic to learn he understood their meaning. So the scholar boldly proclaimed: "Not only do I understand the words, but I understand the meaning as well!"

The woman's celebration came to a screeching halt and her elation quickly turned to anguish. She began sobbing and pulling at her hair. "Why are you so upset?" Naropa asked, completely bewildered by her behavior.

"You are a learned scholar, so when you say you understand the words of the teachings that's true," she said despondently. "But saying you understand the meaning is a lie. You have not attained authentic realization."

Taken aback, Naropa asked what he could do to realize the meaning of teachings. She told him to seek out her brother, a yogi name Tilopa, who could help him experience the truth of the words he studied. Naropa left the confines of the university in search of the yogi. Tilopa put Naropa through twelve excruciating trials. In the end, the scholar learned to let go of his igoic concepts and gained experiential realization. Tilopa instructed him:

> Don't control. Let go and rest naturally.
> Let what binds you go and freedom is not in doubt.
> When you look into space, seeing stops.
> Likewise, when mind looks at mind,
> The flow of thinking stops and you come
> to the deepest awakening.

Like the dakini that confronted Naropa, Erma would continually challenge her students to go beyond words to understand their meaning. "What's that you're sitting on?" she once asked a student.

"Uh, a chair," he replied.

"How do you know it's a chair?" she nudged.

"Well, it has legs and a seat," he answered.

"So do you. Are you a chair?" Erma prodded.

"Well, no," the student admitted.

"OK. So is it a chair or is it called a chair?" she asked pointedly.

"I guess it's just called a chair," he responded.

"If you look beyond that label, what is it that you are sitting on? Where did it come from? How did it get here? Investigate this," Erma encouraged.

As she opened up the question to the group, suggestions percolated. It's wood. More than that, it is a tree, which means it is part of a forest. It is also soil, sunshine, rain, and the wind. It is a home to animals and insects. It is the saw and logger who cut the trees down. It is the truck and driver that transported the trees to the mill and the fuel that powered the vehicle. It is the machines and the factory workers who built it, and the electricity they used. It is the people who sold it at the store and the customer who bought it. "Really, I guess it is connected with everything," a student interjected.

"Yes, it is, and so are we," she agreed. "So, let me ask you again, what are you sitting on?"

"I am sitting on everything," the student concluded.

"Good. Now, can you *feel* that?" she asked. "Can you open to genuine knowing and appreciation for how we are all interconnected? Be with that understanding."

CHAPTER 8
Loving Power

Love alone is capable of uniting living beings
in such a way as to complete and fulfill them,
for it alone takes them and joins them
by what is deepest in themselves.
— *Pierre Teilhard de Chardin*

TIBET'S YARLUNG DYNASTY GREW the Himalayan nation into a regional superpower in the first millennium of the Common Era. The empire's military prowess was feared throughout Asia, and in the eighth century, it was Tibet which controlled much of western China. During military campaigns that continued for a hundred years, Tibet seized the Chinese provinces of Gansu, Sichuan, and northern Yunnan. When the Chinese emperor failed to pay his annual tribute, the army of Tibet's King Trisong Detsen captured the capital city of his rival. This leader is revered by Tibetans for a different reason, though.

King Trisong Detsen helped firmly plant the Buddhist tradition in Tibet by overcoming fierce resistance in his homeland. First, he brought the famed Indian Buddhist scholar Shantarakshita to the Land of Snow. Under the king's direction, Shantarakshita led a massive effort to translate the vast Buddhist cannon from Sanskrit into the Tibetan language. He also started construction of Tibet's first Buddhist monastery, called Samye, near the banks of the Yarlung Tsangpo River.

The monastery project encountered a mountain of obstacles, however, and the building inexplicably collapsed several times during construction. Shantarakshita concluded the problems resulted from interference by demonic spirits and the malicious incantations of Tibetan black magicians. The abbot advised the king to call upon Padmakara, a renowned Buddhist tantric adept, to pacify the problems.

On his way to Samye, Padmakara is said to have overpowered countless malevolent beings in the Himalayas, binding the obstructers under oath to protect Buddhist teachings rather than harm them. Once he arrived at Samye, Padmakara—also known as Padmasambhava and Guru Rinpoche—neutralized negative energies, enabling the monastery to be swiftly completed.

Tibet's King Trisong Detsen and Queen Yeshe Tsogyal became close disciples of Padmakara. By following his guidance, they and many other Tibetan students cultivated the seed of their awakened nature to full fruition. Together, they launched a revolution that transformed Tibet from a land of ferocious marauders to a haven for accomplished meditators for the next 1,200 years.

THE PSYCHIATRIST M. SCOTT PECK challenged the pervasive allure and inevitable disappointment of the igo's promise of easy living in his breakaway bestseller *The Road Less Travelled.* He opened his book with the reminder "life is difficult," explaining that a failure to understand and accept this basic truth pits us in a struggle against the essential nature of the human condition. Peck commented that his diagnosis aligns with the Buddha's First Noble Truth which describes the root of our suffering as a form of delusional dissatisfaction with what is.

Peck shocked his peers in psychiatry and publishing by focusing his follow-up book on a scientifically taboo topic: the nature of evil. Investigating the subject as both a psychiatrist and devoted Christian, Peck came to see evil manifest in people as an extreme and malignant form of narcissism. As a pattern of activity, he defined evil as the intentional use of power to harm others and obstruct their spiritual growth.

Peck concluded that malignant narcissists have profoundly damaged self-worth. However, rather than face the agonizing inner pain and confusion, awareness of it is aggressively suppressed. Narcissists then seek sustenance externally to fill their inner void. An essential strategy is to create a personality facade to gain attention and admiration from others.

The pattern moves from maladaptive igoism to evil when a narcissist comes to relish power and pleasure derived from hurting others. Malignant narcissists therefore lead double lives with a public persona that is accepted or admired and a private pathology that is exploitive and manipulative. Because of the duplicity and falsehoods, Peck came to call those who behave this way "people of the lie."

Interestingly, experiments conducted decades after Peck's work may help prove his point. A group of undergraduate women at an American university completed standard psychological tests measuring narcissistic personality traits and levels of self-esteem. Then, the researchers split the participants into two groups. Both were administered another self-esteem survey, but one group was connected to lie-detector equipment and told their responses would be monitored for truthfulness.

For women with low scores on the narcissistic scale, measures of self-esteem remained the same whether they were connected to the lie detector or not. However, women with high levels of narcissism reported lower levels of self-esteem when they believed the researchers knew whether they were being honest. In other words, narcissists changed their story under the perceived light of truth to avoid being identified as people of the lie.

"The evil hate the light—the light of goodness that shows them up, the light of scrutiny that exposes them, the light of truth that penetrates their deception," Peck contended. "They are continually engaged in sweeping the evidence of their evil under the rug of their own consciousness." Further, because having their flaws exposed is so excruciating, people of the lie may actively seek to "destroy the light, the goodness, the love in order to avoid the pain of such self-awareness." Even if that light is in their own children.

Beyond a simple lack of sensitivity needed to provide essential nurturing, malignant parents actively undermine their children's well-being to enhance their own. Tragically, children traumatized in this way are poised to repeat the pattern.

"I did not come to bring peace, but a sword," Jesus forcefully told his disciples. "For I came to set a man against his father, and a daughter against her mother, and a daughter-in-law against her mother-in-law; and a man's enemies will be the members of his household. He who loves father or mother more than me is not worthy of me."

The intent of Jesus's warning was not to encourage violence in his name but to subdue it. Because peace is the natural condition of one in perfect union with God's love, Jesus didn't need to bring a plate full of peace to dish out. Rather, he was willing to exert loving power to cut through the full spectrum of delusion—mundane igo to malignant evil—which separates us from awareness of ever-present peace and love. In the context of family, when evil is present, there is often a tendency to turn a blind eye to "keep the peace." However, the failure to confront evil does not result in peace, it undermines realization of its genuine presence.

WALKING ACROSS A SHOPPING mall parking lot in Columbus, Ohio, Paul Linden was unexpectedly stopped by a woman he had never met before. "Who are you? You don't walk like other people," she asked. The woman explained she was a psychologist and had noticed him walking the halls of the nearby university where he earned his Ph.D. His movement appeared so fluid and balanced that it left a lasting impression. She wanted to know how he accomplished it.

Linden shared that he had trained for many years in aikido, the non-violent Japanese martial art, becoming a master teacher. He also extensively studied body mechanics and practiced movement methods. She asked Linden if he could apply what he learned to help survivors of childhood abuse. She hoped an embodied process of self-awareness and empowerment could serve as a powerful complement to psychotherapy. With Linden's approval, she began sending him clients.

Working with survivors of childhood abuse over the next decade, Linden found the experience of powerlessness—being unable to protect one's body and self—to be a fundamental wound. Compared to adults, children are powerless, lacking the physical strength, skills, and life experience needed to live independently. For their health, safety, and well-being children need loving adults to protect and nurture them. When adults do so, a child's underlying sense of powerlessness is virtually invisible. As our children grow with such security, they develop through successive cycles of challenge and mastery, becoming more confident, capable, and powerful in the process.

When a child is violated by an adult who is supposed to protect him, the powerlessness that was hidden is laid excruciatingly bare. Following the fear, pain, rage, and despair resulting from the violation, an abused child must find a way to traverse the terrifying terrain. Because he does not have enough power to directly ensure his own safety, he may employ strategies that make him feel like he does.

Although a child is usually unable to change the toxic situation he is living in, he can alter his perception of it. To cope, he may live as if the abuse didn't happen, restricting awareness of the painful memories, body sensations, and feelings. Eventually, this numbing process may evolve to take the form of self-anesthetization through drug or alcohol abuse. Or, he may seek to end his identification with the role of a helpless victim by becoming a controlling aggressor. While there are many indirect coping strategies, they are all based on the deep-seated belief—developed through actual experience—that he lacked the power needed to ensure his safety and well-being.

Linden explains he learned: "The way to break through the logjam of the indirect survival habits is to learn real power. Warmhearted power changes everything. Responding to a threat by speaking the truth, by voicing your feelings and needs, saying NO and making that stick—that is what renders the indirect coping strategies unnecessary. Being able to take direct action and succeed … that is what creates real safety. However, it is important that the power you acquire be loving. Power without love is brutal and abusive. Power with love is healing."

This is what Linden teaches his clients to do through martial arts training and by cultivating awareness of their body's present response to past traumatic experiences. "Powerlessness is constriction of breath, tensing of muscles, shrinking of posture. Powerlessness involves patterns of body sensation, posture, and movement which are small and uneven. They are constricted or collapsed, and they are lopsided or twisted," Linden explains. By comparison: "Power is a state of expansiveness and symmetry. The empowered, centered state is open, bright, vigorous, soft, smooth, stable, fluid, massive, light, balanced, and even. This is at once a physical, emotional, and spiritual state."

Mastery is developed by acting decisively and effectively in this state of loving power, rather than resting passively in a feel-good experience or lashing out in anger. To ensure his clients can truly walk the talk, Linden creates physically and emotionally safe conditions that help simulate the original traumatic situation, offering survivors the chance to face their demons and defeat them.

GROWING UP IN A JEWISH FAMILY in Great Britain, the pioneering Autism researcher Simon Baron-Cohen learned from his father about the horrors committed by Germany's Nazi regime. One particular description of the

Holocaust haunted him—the Nazis had made lampshades and bars of soap from the bodies of their victims. This visceral image of turning people into objects was unfathomable to the seven-year-old boy.

When Baron-Cohen turned his attention to investigating the origins of human cruelty, the notion of "evil" as a cause offered a scientifically unsatisfying explanation. The key, he concluded, was empathy erosion. Somehow, natural feelings of empathy for another's suffering must be shut down in those who willfully harm others. Reviewing the latest neuroscientific research, he theorized the presence of an "empathy circuit" in the human brain that when turned off, enabled terrible cruelty.

Baron-Cohen defines empathy as our ability to identify what someone else is thinking or feeling and to respond to their thoughts and feelings with an appropriate emotion. This requires that we suspend an exclusively self-minded focus and integrate awareness of the needs of both self and other. Without this capacity to connect with more than me, we are trapped within the self-absorbed igo and care only about pursuing our own desires.

We all fall somewhere along the empathy spectrum, Baron-Cohen contends. People who are deeply compassionate operate at the high end of the empathy scale, while those who are deemed evil live on the low end at "zero degrees of empathy."

While Peck focused exclusively on the malignant narcissist, Baron-Cohen added those suffering in the grip of borderline and antisocial personality disorders to his

zero-empathy group. And, he points to insecure attachment and childhood abuse as key contributors to the
development of these zero-empathy personalities. When
the two factors occur in combination, it is a double-
whammy for the developing child. Without a secure base,
resiliency in the face of abuse is significantly reduced, as
is the ability to manage turbulent feelings arising from the
trauma.

Baron-Cohen, it turns out, is a Fellow at the University of Cambridge's Trinity College, where John Bowlby
studied psychology and medicine. Baron-Cohen considers
Bowlby's attachment theory to be remarkable because it
made predictions about transgenerational effects that have
been proven repeatedly through decades of research.
Moreover, attachment security accurately predicts not just
how emotionally well-adjusted a child will be as an adult,
but also their moral development. Whether our empathy
circuit operates as intended is influenced by the way our
compassionate nature is nurtured.

THE SANSKRIT NAME PADMAKARA translates literally as
"lotus born" and describes the spiritual master's mystical
birth. Esoteric accounts explain that Padmakara descended
to earth in the form of a golden *vajra*—an indestructible
scepter—and landed in the heart of a large lotus flower in
a sacred lake in the hidden land of Oddiyana. He emerged
from the flower as a radiant eight-year old boy and was
adopted by the king, bypassing the potential pains and

pitfalls of a conventional human pregnancy, birth, infancy, and early childhood.

Padmakara's name and early narrative offer a meaningful metaphor. The lotus symbolizes our heart and mind's primordially pure nature. Just as the lotus is born from a seed in the mud and muck of a lakebed, our awakened nature can completely blossom in the sludge of earthly suffering and confusion. The vajra represents the indestructability and power of our true nature. The Buddhist teachings that the lotus-born guru Padmakara brought to Tibet are known as Vajrayana—also called Tantra or Secret Mantra—the path that swiftly reveals our already-present awakened nature. "If you know me," Padmakara reminded his student Yeshe Tsogyal, "you will find me dwelling in the heart of every being."

The essential aspects of this path include cleansing our obscured igoic perception, cultivating supportive spiritual conditions and connections, as well as developing our intrinsic capacity for clarity. The catalysts for this process of unfolding, Padmakara taught, are fervent compassion for the suffering we and all ordinary beings experience, devotion to the awakened beings who guide us, and diligence in spiritual practice.

Yeshe Tsogyal exquisitely embodied these qualities on a rugged journey to complete awakening. That she did so as a young woman in a medieval patriarchal society is a testament to her tenacity.

Born the daughter of a provincial Tibetan governor, Tsogyal's beauty attracted an onslaught of interested suitors when she reached the age of twelve. Unable to decide among the two leading candidates, Tsogyal's father tossed her out of the house, telling the men that she would belong to whoever caught her. The minister of a neighboring governor reached her first and was declared the winner of the contest.

As the minister grabbed Tsogyal by the hair, she held her ground, literally. It is said she dug her feet into a boulder, as if stepping into soft clay, becoming as unshakable as a mountain. Outraged by her audacity, the minister tore off her clothes, lashed her with a metal-pronged whip, and beat her until she was mangled and bloody. Weakened by the torment, Tsogyal eventually acquiesced and left with him. That evening at the minister's encampment she prayed fervently for help, her tears mixing with the blood of her wounds.

Miraculously, the men fell asleep at the campfire after a round of beer and Tsogyal fled under the cover of night. She hid in a deep ravine, living on foraged fruit and clothing herself with moss from the trees. She was eventually found and captured by a force of three hundred men—this time commanded by the losing suitor.

With a regional war ready to break out among the allies of the enraged husbands-to-be, Tsogyal's father offered her as a bride to King Trisong Detsen. The king accepted and dispatched an army of nine hundred soldiers, overpowering the suitors' troops and restoring calm to the area. Honoring the new queen's inner strength and intelligence, the king brought her teachers to study reading and grammar, as well as the arts and sciences.

With Padmakara, Tsogyal mastered Buddhist philosophy, complex rituals, and meditation practices. Along the way Tsogyal awakened immense spiritual power. Later, it is said she actually became the king's protector and helped subdue malevolent sorcerers and spirits threatening Tibet's early Buddhist practitioners.

Though Tsogyal and other Tibetans were awed by Padmakara's abilities, he told them not to become fixated on his magical feats. The source of his strength and fearlessness was awareness of our mind's true nature. Padmakara explained: "Within the empty mind essence, beyond concepts, neither gods nor demons exist. Whichever magical trickery you display before me, I am not moved the slightest. There is no way you can destroy the nature of mind."

While Jesus said he came with a sword, Padmakara arrived in Tibet with a *kila*. A three-sided ritual dagger, the kila penetrates the three poisons of igo that afflict our hearts and minds—ignorance, grasping, and aversion—and subdues harmful interference.

Padmakara did not come to the Land of Snow with a cavalier or condescending attitude aimed at converting native heathens. With discernment, he recognized that a branch of the indigenous Tibetan tradition was completely harmonious with the teachings of the Buddha he practiced. However, he also observed the presence of an element that was harmful. He told the king to protect those of the light and their teachings, but banish those of the dark to the borderlands.

With his kila Padmakara divided the larger Tibetan family. More importantly he helped his disciples break through the igo patterns that separated them from their always-present, yet unrecognized, true nature.

CHAPTER 9
Breaking the Mold

To help break the mold that binds the mind and to
disturb the sleeping that they might awaken themselves.
—*Erma Pounds, when asked her life's purpose*

THE TWELTH-CENTURY TIBETAN BUDDHIST master Dusum
Khyenpa profoundly changed the course of history in
Tibet by initiating the practice of intentional
reincarnation. Before dying in 1193, the 83-year-old lama
shared a letter with a close disciple predicting the time,
place, and details of his next birth.

A child matching the description was born in 1206
and recognized as Dusum Khyenpa's reincarnation. The
child, Karma Pakshi, became known as "Karmapa,"
meaning "being of enlightened activity." A stream of
successive Karmapa incarnations has continued in Tibet
ever since with most offering precise predictions of how,
when, and where they would be reborn.

Through such living examples Tibetan Buddhists
came to believe a spiritual adept with complete awareness

of the mind's awakened nature can break through the limits of conventional space and time, allowing them to both influence and recognize the circumstances of their next birth. The master's motivation for doing so is to continue benefitting beings through an uninterrupted flow of compassionate activity and service. The lineage of Dalai Lama incarnations is currently the best-known example of this Tibetan tradition.

His Holiness the 16th Karmapa, Ranjung Rigpe Dorje, was born in 1924 and fifty years later became one of the first Tibetan Buddhist lineage leaders to travel to the United States. While in Boulder, Colorado in 1974, the Karmapa surprised his hosts by insisting he visit the Grand Canyon and Hopi people of Arizona. Obliging his interest, the Karmapa's hosts rented a gold Cadillac and a small caravan of cars hit the road.

The driver recounted that upon their arrival to the Hopi mesas, the red-robed Karmapa was greeted by a village leader. Through a translator, the Karmapa asked how the Hopi were doing. "Not too good," the leader replied. "We haven't had rain in seventy-three days." Expressing deep concern for their plight, the Karmapa reassured him, "I will do something for you."

The Karmapa started chanting a prayer, which continued as he climbed back into the Cadillac to travel to the motel where he would be staying. Small clouds soon formed, intensifying into a dark, foreboding sky. The Karmapa's driver recalled:

> We rolled into the motel parking lot … He got out and walked to his motel room where another attendant stood ready to open the door. I watched his back as he disappeared into the room. At the very instant that the door clicked shut behind him, there was an eruption of thunder and lightning like I've never seen before in my life. Crash! Boom! The most dramatic display you could imagine. And then the rain started coming down hard. Buckets of it. Sheets and torrents of it. It went on and on like that, splashing down on the roof of the Cadillac with the power and intensity of a waterfall.

Celebrating the end of the two-and-half-month drought, the headline of the local Hopi newspaper the following day declared: "Tibetan Chief Brings Rain." Invited to perform a spiritual ceremony by Hopi leaders, the Karmapa donned a red hat typical of his lineage and bestowed a blessing of the Buddha of compassion.

Grateful for the ceremony, some Hopi shared their belief that the Karmapa's visit was the fulfillment of an ancient prophecy that predicted a long-lost brother from the East would arrive to provide help when desperately needed. This brother, "when he comes, will be all powerful and will wear a red cap or red cloak" and "belong to no religion but his very own."

Following her intuition about the Karmapa's Arizona travel plans, Erma Pounds sent two of her students to meet his entourage at the Grand Canyon and invite them to visit Phoenix. During an impromptu gathering in the home of another one of her students she received a telephone call to their unlisted number. "Hello. This is the secretary to His Holiness Karmapa. We plan to visit your home tomorrow," explained a gentleman with a commanding British-Indian accent.

"Sure, come on down. We'll have an orgy," Erma deadpanned, thinking the call was a prank by one of her students.

"Excuse me, madam?" the gentleman responded, apparently bewildered by the offer.

Realizing it actually was the Karmapa's secretary on the line, she quickly apologized for the quip and warmly invited them to visit. In addition to the Karmapa, Bardor Tulku Rinpoche, and other Tibetan lamas, she was told students of Chögyam Trungpa Rinpoche would be coming. Also on the guest list were Freda Bedi (the first European woman to take ordination as a Tibetan Buddhist nun) and Barbara Pettee, who helped sponsor the Karmapa's U.S. tour.

The gold Cadillac carrying the 16th Karmapa and a half-dozen other cars arrived at Erma's house the following day. The students she had sent to the Grand Canyon followed the caravan to Phoenix and were baffled as the Cadillac made a beeline to Erma's home without directions. She greeted the Karmapa with her husband and students. They were mesmerized as the Karmapa appeared to walk from the car across the front yard without his feet touching the ground. Noticing the group gaping at his airborne feet, the Karmapa laughed, stepped down on to the grass, and walked over to meet them.

While such extraordinary occurrences seem far-fetched to our conventional concepts of reality, they are commonplace in other traditions. Masters who spend decades consciously cultivating the full power of their awakened nature are believed to manifest their realization in potent ways which benefit others. Daniel Goleman, a former *New York Times* science writer and author of the bestsellers *Emotional Intelligence* and *Social Intelligence*, explains about such intensive meditation training:

> Science has now verified how powerful just three years of [meditation] retreat can be in sharpening mental faculties. We can only guess what 20 or 30 years might do. From that perspective, we might well suspend our judgments about the seeming 'miraculous' powers routinely ascribed to these Tibetan masters of the past. Who knows what might be possible for a mind so highly and exquisitely trained?

During a private discussion in Erma's home, the Karmapa explained that their meeting resulted from a connection formed in a previous lifetime. Although her spiritual teaching style appeared unorthodox to some, the Karmapa encouraged her to continue. "What you teach your students here, in my tradition, we call Vajrayana," he explained. Some 30 years later this crazy wisdom mother would become my teacher.

THERE IS AN OLD STORY ABOUT a king who was deeply devoted to the welfare of his people. One night he awoke in a cold sweat, shaken by a prophetic dream. In his vision a strange rain fell upon the kingdom, polluting the water supply. Everyone who drank the tainted water soon spiraled into insanity. When the king rose the next morning, he instructed servants to fill vats of pure water and lock them in a palace storeroom for safekeeping.

A few days later the king's vision came true, and as the polluted rain descended, his subjects began to lose their wits. The king drank from his private supply of unsullied water and managed to stay sane. However, as the situation degenerated, the sober king became somber. He was no longer able to understand his subjects—their thoughts, feelings, and experiences had become incomprehensible. Likewise, his behavior completely vexed them. Before long the king raised a glass of the contaminated water to his lips and gulped it down.

Reflecting on the story, some say the king threw in the towel from a sense of weariness, loneliness, or a lack of moral fiber. Others view this king as an embodiment of extreme altruism. Because he so loved his people this compassionate king fearlessly chose to dive into the melee. Which interpretation resonates more with you—an epic anchored in clinging to personal sanity and separateness or one embracing extreme empathy, connection, and chaos?

The king knows his true nature—and that of all beings—is primordially pure, indestructible, and ever-present. Understanding his true nature cannot be tainted by dancing with the deranged, the king refuses to let the fear of pain or confusion snuff out the spark of his naturally arising compassion. The king takes the plunge to directly experience the delusion of those he needs to guide. He is willing to feel how they feel and do what they do, trusting he will ultimately reconnect with his true nature and help others do the same. Of course, it goes without saying that the heroic king may feel lost for a time upon entering a matrix of misery.

In the sci-fi film *The Matrix*, Thomas Anderson, lives a double-life as a corporate software coder and covert hacker known as Neo. Dissatisfaction with his life experience opens the door to a radical search for truth. True to the adage "when the student is ready the teacher will appear" he meets his guide, Morpheus, who explains:

> Let me tell you why you're here. You're here because you know something. What you know you can't explain, but you feel it. You've felt it your entire life, that there's something wrong with the world. You don't know what it is, but it's there, like a splinter in your mind, driving you mad. It is this feeling that has brought you to me. Do you know what I'm talking about?

Once Anderson answers "Yes" everything changes. Morpheus directly introduces Neo to the nature of reality, breaking the mold that binds his mind. Neo then embarks on a hero's journey, traversing the badlands of his own fear, anger, and despondence to become a master of the matrix for the benefit of all. Along the way Neo learns that what he perceives to be "wrong with the world" is in fact the perfect catalyst for awakening. Without the beeping of that incessant and irritating alarm, he would push the snooze button to keep slumbering in confusion and complacency. Like Neo, if our wish is to wake up, the current conditions couldn't be better.

WHILE WORKING AS A technology journalist I once interviewed a top Internet engineer who served at NASA earlier in his career. A favorite saying among his rocket scientist colleagues had shaped his outlook on life: "With enough thrust anything can fly." Forget perfectionism. Even a spacecraft with aerodynamics worse than a Winnebago can be put into orbit with a big enough boost.

The foundational practices of the Vajrayana Buddhist tradition (called *ngondro* in Tibetan) are formulated to create enough thrust to free us from the gravitational grip of the igo and propel us into the orbit of an awakened teacher who can help us connect with our true nature.[†]

It doesn't matter if this spiritual guide is an under-the-radar-yogi who stocks the shelves at the local supermarket or a famous teacher from Tibet. In Vajrayana, the person who directly introduces you to the true nature of your mind is your root guru—regardless of their reputation. Because of their essential role in our journey, meeting one's root guru is the same as being with the Buddha in person.

The ngondro begins with four contemplations that inspire us to commit to and persevere in deep spiritual

---

[†]A very brief overview of the ngondro practices are provided here. In addition to traditional texts, there are several contemporary commentaries available for those interested in diving deeper into the material, including *Not for Happiness: A Guide to the So-Called Preliminary Practices* by Dzongsar Jamyang Khyentse (Shambhala Publications, 2012), and *Ngondro Instructions for Practices in the Termas of Terchen Barway Dorje* by Lama Tashi Topgyal (KPL Publications, 2012).

practice. The first contemplation is appreciating the preciousness and rarity of our human life. Our heart beats a hundred-thousand times a day without being asked. How many of those heartbeats do we experience with gratitude?

Rather than taking our precious human life for granted, we can choose to live with thankfulness. The Buddhist view is that obtaining a human birth defies astronomical odds, like hitting a giant jackpot in a cosmic Powerball drawing. Human beings account for an infinitesimal slice of life on Earth—only one of more than 8 million species. And among humans, being born in a place with basic necessities and freedoms, access to authentic spiritual teachers and teachings, and the time to practice, is rarer still. When these conditions are present in our lives, we are blessed with an optimal spiritual training ground.

The second contemplation is the truth of impermanence. Our life is as fragile as it is precious. It can literally end at any moment. A Tibetan adage captures the sentiment: "Our next breath or next life, which will come first?" In reality, tomorrow is no more than an idea.

The third contemplation is karma, the law of cause and effect. Non-virtuous actions in this and previous lifetimes plant seeds for future suffering. Like a dandelion seed, we could be blown through the winds of space-time to who-knows-where when death comes. There are no guarantees that we will have another opportunity like this one.

The final contemplation is the certainty that any un-enlightened being is bound to suffer. Is it not our deepest desire to find lasting happiness and freedom from the cycle of suffering once and for all? While we have this precious and fragile human life, focusing our efforts on anything but awakening is lunacy.

The inspiration for complete liberation offers the fuel to train in a continuing cycle of meditation practices that fully engage the power of our body, speech, and mind. Called the four extraordinary foundations, the first practice is the generation of bodhicitta and taking refuge. We reaffirm our wholehearted commitment to the most awesome of aspirations—bringing about total freedom for every being in the universe. Then we take refuge from our igos in our true nature through the support of enlightened beings, their teachings, and the community of wakeful spiritual practitioners. The refuge practice involves visualizations and physical prostrations to cut through the igo's pride and resistance.

Up next is a purification practice aimed at clearing away karmic residue and obscurations that create suffering and impede the recognition of our true nature. The third step is an offering practice that connects us with vast gratitude and generosity, magnetizing supportive conditions for our awakening journey. Last but not least is deep devotional practice. With genuine longing, we call out to the lineage of enlightened teachers for blessings to connect us with our already-enlightened nature.

Traditionally, each of these practices is completed 100,000 times—sometimes more or less depending on a lineage teacher's instructions. It is said that through these practices you will meet your Morpheus—the root guru who can guide you to awakening in this lifetime.

Ultimately, the awakening journey is only complicated and uncomfortable from the igo's perspective. Our true nature is merely covered by layers of obscuration that seem to be set in stone. Engaging in the practices of an authentic spiritual lineage is like being handed a hammer and chisel. Carving a massive block of stone is work, requiring skill and stamina. However, whether the work is excruciating or ecstatic depends on the degree to which we identify with the stone or the awakening seed concealed inside.

There is a story of a sculptor who created extraordinarily lifelike figures. "How do you do it?" he was once asked. "I sit quietly with the block until I can see the creature that is trapped inside the stone," the sculptor replied. "Then I use my tools to release it." If we believe we are the block of stone, each blow of the chisel is experienced with fear or resentment at the loss. However, when we connect with the pure being trapped inside, we appreciate the strike of the chisel as an act of liberation that, bit by bit, frees our awakening seed to sprout.

Ngondro and other Vajrayana practices are designed to powerfully sing to the seed of our true nature, crack open the igo's shell, and open space for the flowering of our inherent wisdom and compassion. As painful feelings and experiences inevitably arise on the path, the great Vajrayana master Padmakara (known by Tibetans as Guru Rinpoche) challenged his disciples to embrace them as fuel for awakening. "Let your heart be filled with sadness at this passing world, and this is a crucial point," he counseled.

Rather than suppress our anguish about what is happening or wallow in despair about it, he encouraged meditators to connect with the full power of these emotions. With the wish to awaken for the benefit of all, pray fervently "again and yet again, with deep devotion, tears in your eyes," Padmakara taught. Hearing the cries, he promised to respond "like a mother helpless to resist her darling baby's tears."

The purpose of devotional practice is not to foster a sense of dependence or blind obedience to an outside authority. Instead, it is an invitation to open to our deepest yearnings for freedom and connection. "People ordinarily seek someone else to tell them what to do," my own teacher Erma once counseled. "It is fear that throws responsibility onto someone else. Buddha throws you to yourself."

I RECEIVED THE INSTRUCTIONS and transmission for the ngondro of the Karmapa's Kagyu tradition from a lineage teacher and began practicing intensely. A few months later I met Erma in a penetratingly lucid dream encounter. The dream began as a pleasant visit with a profoundly wise and compassionate friend in her home. But as the full power of her presence unfolded, the igo's conceptual overlays disintegrated into an undivided ground of pure being. As Erma explained there were some specific exercises and practices she wished to share with me, I awoke. I rested in bed with the profound presence she introduced. Any thoughts attempting to make sense of the encounter appeared absurdly feeble compared to the intensity of direct, non-conceptual awareness.

For a mind in the igo's grip, the roaring river of thoughts and feelings overruns subtle awareness. With recognition of unborn awareness, the roar reverses and the presence of awareness engulfs the conditioned thought stream. Clarity of our natural state is extraordinarily vivid and empty—the full spectrum from neon to pastel—infused with cognizance of the intensity of appearance as empty and ephemeral. As conventional reference points collapse, freedom naturally dawns from perceived separateness of self and other, here and there, past and future. Awareness meets the raw, pulsating flow of space, energy, and radiant form in its complete emptiness and fullness.

The appearance of Erma as the catalyst for the dreamtime experience was a complete surprise. I had met her a few times and she seemed to be a kind, albeit eccentric, grandmother. I was aware she was a Kagyu lineage teacher, but didn't feel a strong personal connection. However, as I continued my ngondro practice, the overnight encounters with Erma did as well. After working through my resistance to the obvious, I decided to seek her out in person a month after our first dream meeting.

SING TO THE SEED

I learned Erma would be teaching on a Sunday after-noon at a nonsectarian spiritual gathering hosted by a pair of her students. The advertised lesson was a classic Bud-dhist topic, the three higher trainings (ethical conduct, meditative concentration, and wisdom). However, she covered much broader terrain. She shared instructions from the Dzogchen (Great Perfection) tradition, as well as details about Padmakara, and a hidden valley in Tibet known as Pemakö.[‡]

After the teaching I introduced myself and asked if we could schedule a personal visit to get to know each other better. Erma replied it would be more beneficial to simply attend the weekly teachings at the Buddhist center she directed.

When I arrived at the center for her teaching the fol-lowing week, everything appeared conventional. The altar included traditional statues and offerings, meditation cushions and mats were mindfully arranged in the shrine room, and pictures of Buddhas and lineage masters lined the walls. However, as people filed in and sat for the evening meditation and teaching, rather than reciting lineage prayers, a student started playing guitar. "Who in the room can dance like a monkey?" Erma asked. Several students hopped to their feet and gave it their best shot while singing:

[‡] The Tibetan term Dzogchen, literally "Great Perfection," refers to our unchanging true nature, as well as the methods that nurture its recognition. For more on Pemakö, see *The Heart of the World: A Journey to Tibet's Lost Paradise* by Ian Baker.

> The ego is a monkey,
> swinging from branch to branch.
> Desires, problems, self-centered ideas.
> Just let the ego go. Just watch.
> And then forget that you are there. §

The words were Erma's. The song was one of many she had spontaneously penned to make traditional meditation instructions more accessible to her American students. However, for someone expecting standard Buddhist teachings, the raucous scene was completely disorienting. That was the point, of course, to eviscerate expectations and concepts that obstruct our connection with direct experience.

Erma explained monkey mind impedes awareness of our ever-present awakened nature. The monkey may manifest as conceptualization run amok or emotional hyperactivity that overwhelms our natural clarity. Learning to let this igo monkey go—and the false sense of separation its patterns project—brings us closer to the recognition of our true nature. Like other lineage teachers, she called that nature Buddha Mind or Wisdom Mind.

The next song she had her students sing explained the principle:

> This Buddha Mind, Wisdom Mind
> is not born, nor does it pass away.
> This Buddha Mind, Wisdom Mind
> continuously present and unchanging.
> Vajradhara Dorje Chang.

---

§ The meaning of Erma's "ego" is the same as "igo."

Fortunately, I was familiar enough with Buddhist history not to take the assault on expectations personally. Like the old woman who reeducated Naropa, Erma would tirelessly help her students cut through their concepts about spiritual practice. Sometimes that meant melting our pain and fear with a great mother's love. In other instances, slicing through afflictive patterns like a sword-wielding samurai was her preferred method. In my own case she deftly balanced both. Erma sometimes shared remedial mothering with those who needed it, but was careful for it not to degrade into dependency or igoic indulgence. Beyond working through issues of psychological nurture, her goal was to support the recognition of our true nature.

Nonetheless, our igoic insecurities and conditioning can be stubborn. Despite my direct experience with Erma, her unconventional methods repeatedly fired up my own lingering doubts and anxieties about the authenticity of our connection—whether it was "good enough." Six months after I had been studying with her, a senior Tibetan teacher of the Karmapa's tradition visited our center. During the question and answer session following his talk, I poked and prodded.

"Erma has been sharing Dzogchen teachings. Are there any additional instructions you can offer that would be helpful?" I asked.

"On the subject of Dzogchen," he replied, "there is absolutely nothing I can share that Erma is not already teaching you."

"What if I leave the room?" Erma quipped.

I got the message.

While Erma encouraged her students to passionately pursue their particular path, she continually cautioned against the pitfalls of sectarian bias. Her ecumenical advice was not anchored in a naïve notion of spiritual oneness, but through her actual experience with advanced practitioners of many different traditions. She once shared a poignant example.

Through the centuries there are many accounts of Vajrayana Buddhist and Dzogchen masters with deep realization attaining a "rainbow body" following death. Through this energetic process the master's body progressively shrinks rather than conventionally decomposing. The corpse radiates rainbow light as it becomes ever smaller and eventually dissolves into space, leaving only hair and nails behind. Tibetan Buddhists often assume the phenomenon is unique to their tradition in the Himalayas. However, while Erma was present with one of her Hopi teachers at his time of death, she watched the same rainbow body process unfold as he sat beside the Pinyon pine tree where his mother had buried the placenta from his birth.

To drive home the importance of avoiding narrow-mindedness, Erma once handed me an index card with a reminder about the Buddha's approach to teaching *dharma* or universal truth. Her handwritten note read:

> The Buddha never taught anything sectarian. He taught dharma, which is universal. This universality is what attracts. (Unfortunately, there is frequently attached a sectarian connotation).

No particular spiritual tradition can claim ownership of awakening. The true nature of everyone and everything is primordially pure. This awakened essence cannot be stained or tarnished. No one has more or less. It is not born and does not die. Our hearts may ache with pain or longing, but from this essential ground, everything is fundamentally all right—even the voice of the igo that viscerally rejects this possibility. In the times we are hurting most, ultimately, our true nature is already healed.

Because our awakened essence is continually present, wherever we are, whatever we are doing, we can recognize it. We may be meditating alone in a cave in the Himalayas or changing a poopy diaper in Poughkeepsie, reciting Hail Mary in a gothic cathedral or watching one thrown on Monday Night Football, making love or making lunch, sitting in Starbucks, riding the subway, sleeping, or suffering from loss or illness—anytime or anywhere we can become aware.

In London's subway system, known locally as the Tube or the Underground, the voice of a cheery chap instructs riders to "Mind the Gap!" The automated recording alerts passengers entering or exiting a train of the space between the subway car and station platform. When we carefully observe the happenings within our own mind, it appears busier than rush hour. Within the seemingly endless chatter, however, is boundless vibrant space. Clear awareness of this vivid spaciousness supports recognition of our natural state.

Learning to mind the gap within the hustle and bustle of our thoughts and feelings is a gateway. There is nothing we need to achieve or attain. Rather, we are invited to relax, release our igo identification, and recognize what is.

Awareness of the innate spaciousness of our heart and mind is like the sun blazing in a brilliant blue sky. Anything that appears—clouds, rain, snow, hail, hummingbirds, helicopters, or hot air balloons—comes and goes, yet the sky's nature is unchanged. Likewise, whatever content arises in our mind—worries, fears, fantasies, resentments, cravings, or ah-ha insights—is fleeting.

Like the double helix of our DNA, life's polarities are inexorably intertwined—creation and destruction, anguish and bliss, confusion and clarity. Ideas about life collapse in the face of its actual immensity and intensity. Meeting unborn awareness pulverizes preconceptions, daring us to become fully human and wholeheartedly love life as it is.

CHAPTER 10

Wise Faith

From the very beginning
all the infinite number of beings that exist
have as their essential inherent condition
the perfectly pure state of an enlightened being;
knowing this to be also true of me
I commit myself to supreme realization.
— *Longchenpa*

PRIOR TO HIS DEATH STEVE JOBS designed his own memorial service as meticulously as an Apple product launch. At the end of the event each attendee received a box concealing a final farewell gift. Some thought the box might contain a never-before-seen i-gadget. Apple's founder chose to share a radically different technology: the book *Autobiography of a Yogi* by Paramahansa Yogananda. The spiritual classic served a continual source of inspiration for Jobs, propelling him on a spiritual pilgrimage to India as a young man, motivating him to meditate regularly, and shaping his approach to life and business.

It is a book that can deeply resonate or repel. Yoga-nanda's devotion to his guru—plus his equally passionate and systematic approach to spiritual practice—can set a reader's heart on fire. Or, it can send his or her head fleeing for cover. My wife received the book as a gift from a friend when we were in our twenties. She shared it with me, and like Apple's guru, my response was combustible.

Yogananda's example inspired me to start meditating. However, unlike the contemplative bliss the yogi described, my experience was excruciating. Practicing meditation felt like sitting with the pounding staccato of a conceptual-emotional jackhammer inside my own skull. Resting quietly with my breath for a mere five minutes required an extraordinary act of will. Given my frustrations with meditation, the notion that our essential condition is the perfectly pure state of an enlightened being seemed preposterous. And yet, a potent openness to this possibility propelled me to continue. So did meeting accomplished lamas that genuinely embodied this potential.

Lama is the Tibetan translation of the Sanskrit word guru. The Tibetan prefix "la" means beyond or above, while "ma" is mother. Thus, an authentic lama has realization beyond ordinary beings and cares for them with the love and skill of a great mother.

After I connected with Erma, I learned that the friend who had given my wife the copy of *Autobiography of a Yogi* was herself a student of Erma in her twenties. In the book, Yogananda described the joy of being with his guru: "If I entered the hermitage in a worried or indifferent frame of mind, my attitude imperceptibly changed. A healing calm descended at mere sight of my guru." This was my experience with Erma as well. Being with her felt like coming home in the deepest sense.

Rather than blissing out in his guru's presence, Yogananda worked diligently with his teacher to unravel the conditioning that impeded connection with his own true nature. "For every humbling blow he dealt my vanity, for every tooth in my metaphorical jaw he knocked loose with stunning aim, I am grateful beyond any facility of expression. The hard core of human egotism is hardly to be dislodged except rudely. With its departure, the Divine finds at last an unobstructed channel," Yogananda recounted.

As in the Indian yogic tradition, the guru or lama is the lynchpin of the Buddhist paths of Vajrayana, Mahamudra, and Dzogchen. The lama offers essential oral meditation instructions, corrective guidance, and when the necessary conditions are present, direct introduction to our true nature. However, this introduction can only occur when a student has enough trust to break through the igo's resistance.

An authentic lama or guru never encourages blind faith or idiotic adoration. There is too much at stake. It would be a tragedy of epic proportions if this sacred relationship degraded into personality worship, imbecilic obedience, or authoritarian abuse of any kind. The point is to eviscerate igoic delusion, not reinforce it. When asked how she vetted her own teachers, Erma once shared: "First, I always felt a strong connection with them in my heart. Then, I investigated to be sure they actually walked their talk."

The Buddha explained that faith is critical to the path of awakening. However, he advocated a wise faith rooted in reason and corroborated by direct experience. He encouraged a seeker investigating spiritual teachings and teachers to be like a merchant buying gold. Before putting her money down, she verifies what is advertised as precious is in fact the real thing.

Invariably, if we look carefully we can find unhealthy pathologies playing out with many so-called spiritual gurus and disciples. However, the knee-jerk dismissing of the value of devotional practice is throwing the baby out with the bathwater. It cuts us off from a powerful pathway that can bring about awakening in a single lifetime. We must be vigilant and discerning. However, when we meet the real deal, it is up to us to muster the courage to open our hearts and minds completely to the blessings that are available.

Scrutiny of teachers and teachings can be intense in traditional Buddhist cultures. It is entirely appropriate to investigate a potential teacher for years and seek references before committing to a relationship. More importantly, there is the understanding that the lama is ultimately none other than our own awakened nature in a form we can recognize and relate to. Kalu Rinpoche, one of the great Kagyu yogis of the twentieth century, explained:

> What we call the Buddha, or the lama, is not material in the same way as iron, crystal, gold, or silver are. You should never think of them with this sort of materialistic attitude. The essence of the lama or Buddha is emptiness; their nature, clarity; their appearance the play of unimpeded awareness. Apart from that, they have no real, material form, shape or color whatsoever—like the empty luminosity of space. When we know them to be like that, we can develop faith, merge our minds with theirs, and let our minds rest peacefully. This attitude and practice are most important.

To drive this point home Erma often reminded her students that "the situation is the guru." Whatever arises in our direct experience can help point out the nature of our heart and mind. She once shared the details of an encounter with someone who did not remotely understand this. A woman Erma hardly knew showed up on her doorstep with packed suitcases and rang the doorbell. When Erma opened the door the woman pronounced: "I have heard you are a great spiritual master. I am ready to move in and become your disciple." Rather than welcoming in a new roommate, Erma eventually helped her find psychological counseling.

The Tibetan word for devotion (*mogu*) has a precise meaning. The prefix "mo" refers to longing or yearning while "gu" means respect and eagerness. Yearning in this case means wholeheartedly opening to our desire for complete awakening for all. We trust that we possess this potential and can meet a guide who can help nurture its unfolding. Respecting these fundamentals, we eagerly and responsibly apply ourselves in practice. Rather than worship someone, we make the courageous commitment to do what it takes to become Buddhas ourselves.

Through Erma I was blessed to connect with Bardor Tulku Rinpoche. I have not met a sincerer embodiment of wise faith and genuine compassion. Bardor Tulku was born in 1950 into a nomadic family in Kham, a remote region of eastern Tibet. As a young child he was recognized by the 16th Karmapa as the third incarnation of the nonsectarian Buddhist master Terchen Barway Dorje.

Following the Red Army's invasion of Tibet nine-year-old Bardor Tulku and twelve family members departed on foot for India. The family braved 17,000-foot mountain passes through the Himalayas and finally reached the sweltering jungles of Assam, India. The physical hardship of the journey and the dramatic change in climate extracted their toll. All twelve members of Bardor Tulku's family died in Assam.

The young boy courageously continued onward. He knew that his root guru from many lifetimes, the 16th Karmapa, had fled Tibet in 1951 and established a seat in exile in Sikkim, India. When Bardor Tulku reached the Indian border a sympathetic government officer offered to help him resettle as a refugee in the country. To the officer's disbelief, the young boy declined the offer. He told the officer that from the depths of his heart he knew that even though he had lost his family and home, everything would be fine once he was with his guru.

146

The young Bardor Tulku crisscrossed India's border with Bhutan and eventually made it to Darjeeling in the Indian state of West Bengal. The 16th Karmapa learned of his arrival and arranged for the then twelve-year-old boy to be brought to his seat at Rumtek, Sikkim. For more than a decade Bardor Tulku trained under the 16th Karmapa's direction with other reincarnate Kagyu masters.

Bardor Tulku Rinpoche traveled with the 16th Karmapa on his tours to the U.S in the 1970s. He later relocated to New York and over the next thirty years tirelessly supported the construction of the Karmapa's North American seat. Following visionary advice from his guru, he also married, became a father, and established Kunzang Palchen Ling in New York's Hudson Valley to share the teachings of his personal lineage. Having lived in the United States for more than four decades, he appreciates our culture of extreme spiritual skepticism.

"When gurus say the essence of the path is faith in the guru, it sounds like self-promotion. It sounds suspiciously like a scam," Bardor Tulku noted. "We must understand that what we seek in practice is a meeting of minds. The meeting of the mind of the student and the mind of the guru. For this to happen the guru must be qualified—he or she must be the real thing—and the disciple must have faith."

It is said that enabling this meeting of the minds is like cranking an old-fashioned water pump. For the pump to work it has to be connected to water. When the well is dry, water will not flow even if we pump ourselves to complete exhaustion. This is akin to having devotion for an unqualified guru. On the flip side, a student who lacks faith in an authentic guru is like someone standing in front of a pump connected to a freshwater spring who refuses to push the handle.

The blessings of awakened beings are also likened to sun rays or falling rain. It is up to us to step out into the open to feel them. Buying into the wounded igo's fear and mistrust is like placing a steel dome over a garden. It cuts us off from the vital elements that enable our awakening seed to sprout and grow to fruition.

Because the true nature of the mind we seek to meet is beyond birth and death or a fixed place in space, there are a myriad of ways the meeting can happen. There is no requirement to sit at a lama's feet 24/7 to soak up blessings like a human sponge. If it were a prerequisite for awakening, not many people could walk the path. Very few iPhone's would be in use if Steve Jobs had to build each one by hand in his workshop.

In the Tibetan Buddhist tradition, ngondro and other practices are specifically designed to offer students the opportunity to swiftly travel the path wherever they are. It is essential to receive practice instructions and transmission from a lineage teacher and check in regularly for technical support. Making up your own spiritual path may turn out as well as trying to build your own iPhone and app store.

Devoted commitment to an authentic lama or lineage is not intended to be restrictive, nor foster a sense of division or bias. The goal is to concentrate the energy of blessings to accelerate the awakening process, like starting a fire by focusing sunlight with a magnifying glass. This intense focus is not meant to cut us off from other awakened lineages. The more inclusive we are, the more blessings we can receive.

On a trip to Canada with his root guru Bardor Tulku witnessed a powerful example of the principle. A young Native Canadian man asked the 16th Karmapa a poignant question: "I am an Indian and I don't know Tibetan customs, but I have faith in you. If I pray to you in an Indian way, can you still grant me your blessings and compassion in your Tibetan way?" Without hesitation the Karmapa answered "Yes, definitely."

"I found this very impressive and very significant because the point is that the blessings of Buddhas are available to any being who has faith in them—regardless of what tradition they may choose to practice—or possibly no tradition at all," Bardor Tulku explained.

As the power of wise faith works to unwind the igo, the disruption of our delusion can feel unnerving. The Greek sage Plato exquisitely described our propensity to reflexively recoil from the intensity of truth into the familiarity of our habitual conditioning.

In *The Republic*, Plato's protagonist Socrates paints a harrowing picture of a group of human beings who have spent their lives imprisoned in an underground cave. They have been shackled since childhood, unable to turn their heads, facing a stone wall opposite the mouth of the cave.

A fire blazes upon a ledge behind them, and in front of the fire is a raised walkway. As travelers cross the walkway, their shadows are projected onto the wall in front of the prisoners. "To them," Socrates explains of the prisoners, "the truth would be literally nothing but the shadows of the images."

When the day comes that a liberator unshackles one of the prisoners and walks him toward freedom, the intensity of the sunlight is more than his eyes can bear. He turns his head away from the brilliant glare and back toward the shadows. As his sensitive eyes gradually adjust to the light he comes to see that his view was remarkably restricted.

On the journey from our caves of delusion most of us will be led back into the shadows by our inner hibernator. When we remain committed to the process, our lineage guides appear again and again to help turn us toward the light of liberation.

The awakening journey is a kind of rebirth. If we were lovingly nurtured during the vulnerability of infancy and childhood, trusting this rebirth process may come naturally. We know that we are supported and it will turn out just fine in the end. If we were neglected or rejected, the opposite may be true. When flowing through a resonant rebirthing process, unprocessed suffering may explode into our consciousness. As excruciating as it feels, it offers a tremendous opportunity. By connecting with our compassionate nature and allowing that to soothe our deepest suffering, we can meet nurturing we missed.

Our typical relationship with suffering is to follow it as if it were our leader or despise it as if it were our enemy. We either join up and run with it or try to annihilate it. There is another way. We can open to our suffering and experience it with loving awareness. It is liberated by letting it be and recognizing its empty nature. Rather than searching for someone to love us, we come to realize that we are the love we seek. Our nature is already complete and whole. It always has been and always will be. What fluctuates is our recognition of it.

Ultimately, wise faith and devotion are profound forms of compassion. They give birth to the inspiration to fearlessly ask for what matters most and the perseverance to overcome resistance that arises in response. When the igo has us feeling terrified, ashamed, or in the grip of desire-gone-wild, devotion and compassion embolden us to continue walking the path of awakening.

May our effort on the journey help every living being nurture awareness of our unchanging true nature.

Afterword: Meditation

Nothing ever becomes real till it is experienced.
— John Keats

IN WISDOM TRADITIONS THE POINT of sharing words is to lead us beyond them. Through spiritual practice we are cultivating awareness that is non-conceptual. While the intellect is a useful tool in many circumstances, it is unsuited for this particular task, like trying to saw a log with a screwdriver.

The literal meaning of meditation is cultivating familiarity of our actual condition. Progressive instructions for five meditation practices distilled from the Buddhist tradition follow. It is important to remember that how we practice is as important as what we practice. To ensure the "what" aligns with the "how," engage in these practices with what are called "the three goodnesses."

Goodness in the beginning: Trusting in the basic goodness of our true nature, we make a choice to seek safe harbor from igo through the support of awakened beings, their teachings, and the community of wakeful spiritual practitioners. As our scope of concern expands from me to we, we naturally connect with the heartfelt

153

aspiration that our practice brings about total freedom for all beings who are suffering.

Goodness in practice: We practice with a felt sense of openness and loving-kindness for all (including ourselves). Free of judgement or labeling, we recognize the illusory nature of igo, its delusional misperceptions, and unwind the patterns that bind.

Goodness in completion: We dedicate all the virtue and positive energy generated through our practice to the complete awakening and ultimate well-being of all beings.

Start each practice with the goodness in the beginning, engage with the goodness during the practice, and conclude your meditation session with the goodness in completion.

1. Calm Abiding

Calm abiding is resting fully in the present moment. My own teacher beautifully described it as "abiding calmly and allowing genuine meditation to naturally arise." As a practice, calm abiding is training in both attention and intention.

Sit comfortably in a chair or cross-legged on a meditation cushion. Start with the felt intention of goodness in the beginning. Rest naturally with your spine straight, but not stiff, and hands open in your lap. With eyes open, relax your vision while gazing over your nose to a point on the floor about a body's length in front of you. With attention gently centered on the breath, allow your body and mind to relax. Thoughts, feelings, and sensations will naturally arise in your field of awareness. Trust each arising is fine as it is, let it be, and gently return your attention to the breath.

Know that how we are practicing is as important as what we are practicing. Check that you are practicing with a sense of humor, openness, and loving-kindness— without judgement or fixation. Thoughts and feelings are a natural part of the human experience. Rather than trying to stop them or becoming fascinated with them as they arise, welcome them while letting them be. If the thought or feeling arises that the way we are practicing is some-how "not good enough," open to that too. Because goodness is our basic nature, our sincere effort is always good enough.

As you begin training in calm abiding, it is often helpful to practice for a short time, many times. Start with as little as five minutes, and as your capacity to connect with the present moment deepens, gradually expand your practice time. When possible, end a session while connected with a sense of freshness and part with your practice as friends. Conclude with goodness in completion by dedicating the virtue.

2. Open Presence

Start with goodness in the beginning and a period of calm abiding with the breath as an object of awareness. When relaxed and grounded in natural breathing, let go of the breath as a focal point. Rest openly and naturally in the fullness of the present moment as it is.

As a support for deepening your connection with open presence, bring awareness to the space in the open palms of your hands. In your direct experience, observe the texture of that space. Is the space within the palms still or vibrant? If there is awareness of the vibrant energy of space, rest with it. As resting stabilizes, allow awareness of vibrant space to gradually expand from the area within the palms to the space between both hands. Observe the texture of that space. As that recognition stabilizes, allow awareness to extend to the space between the arms, within the abdomen and chest, within the neck and head, and finally within the hips, legs, feet, and the ground.

With awareness of vibrant space, let go of any point of reference within the body. Relaxed, clear, alert, and fully present, abide naturally and freely. Notice the vividness of experience, the sharpness and intensity of awareness itself. Recognize that sounds, sights, smells, sensations, thoughts, and feelings spontaneously arise from and dissolve into this vibrant expanse, like waves forming from and falling back into the sea.

Know that whatever arises in your field of awareness does not alter the essence of space or awareness itself, just as the nature of the sky is unchanged by passing clouds. Rest awareness naturally, allowing the clouds of thoughts, feelings, and sensations to flow through the unchanging sky-like expanse of mind. Conclude with goodness in completion. Be aware of this vivid spaciousness when you move your body and arise from your seat.

3. Asking and Receiving

Start with goodness in the beginning and a period of calm abiding or open presence practice. Connect with the deep yearning in your own heart for complete liberation in this brief and precious lifetime, allowing the expansion of that feeling to encompass all beings in the same situation.

With this heartfelt longing call out for the support of all awakened beings in the fulfillment of your aspiration. The energy of that intention coalesces as a translucent sphere of white light resting an arm's length above your head. The sphere of light then radiates in all directions into the expanse of space, magnetizing the energy and blessings of all enlightened beings. Their compassionate response is swift and unconditional. Their blessings flow back to the sphere in the form of light. Know that this sphere is the inseparability of your awakened nature and that of all enlightened beings.

In response to the yearning in your own heart for complete liberation for all, the blessings of awakened body, speech and mind flow from the sphere of light above into your body. White light flows into the center of your forehead. Red light flows into your throat. Blue light flows into in the heart-center of your chest. Then, the sphere of light above you descends through the top of your head, continuing along the spine, through the throat, coming to rest in your heart center. Know that you have received the blessings of awakened body, speech, and mind. Your awakened essence and that of the enlightened ones is inseparable. Rest naturally with awareness. Conclude with goodness in completion.

4. Taking and Sending

Start with goodness in the beginning and a period of calm abiding, open presence, and asking and receiving. Resting naturally, imagine that your awakened nature and that of all fully enlightened beings appears as a sphere of white light an arm's length above your head. Bring awareness to the center of your heart and connect with the felt aspiration that all beings (including yourself) become free from all suffering forever. Allow this aspiration to grow into the passionate resolve to make it happen.

As your heart opens, the ball of white light above descends downward through the top of your head, continuing through the throat and coming to rest in your heart center. Know that your true nature, represented by the sphere of light in your heart space, is infinitely wise and compassionate and has the power to alleviate all suffering.

Resting in the loving power of that noble heart light, invite any aspect of yourself that is suffering to appear before you. If it is helpful, you can start by seeing yourself as a baby with the fundamental need for unconditional caring and nurturing.

As you inhale, breathe in any suffering your baby self is experiencing. You feel this as heaviness and see it as dark smoke being drawn from the baby into the ball of light in your heart center. Because this heart light is so powerful, the smoke dissolves on contact. As you exhale, white light, joy, love, and spaciousness flows from the ball of white light with your outbreath into the baby. Breath by breath, as the baby's suffering dissipates, she becomes radiant, happy, and peaceful.

If an image of yourself appears from a different age in your life, practice taking and sending in the same way through the light in the heart center. The process is very natural, just as a tree takes in carbon dioxide and shares oxygen. As you become more comfortable and confident in the practice, extend the taking to others to whom you feel close, indifferent, or adversarial. If at any time you feel overwhelmed by the suffering encountered, return awareness to the heart light and practice taking and sending for this aspect of your suffering self until it finds freedom. When completing the session, allow the heart light to dissolve into space and rest naturally. Conclude with the goodness in completion.

5. At the Time of Death

Through long-term practice with the three goodnesses, calm abiding, open presence, asking and receiving, and taking and sending, we can cultivate our capacity for equanimity with intense experiences, including illness and death.

Like birth, death is a natural part of life. Through the practice of intentional reincarnation over the past nine hundred years, meditation masters of the Tibetan Buddhist tradition have repeatedly demonstrated that death is as much a beginning as an ending. My own teachers often shared a simple and direct practice for our time of death.

Connect with our noble-hearted aspiration for the complete awakening of all and our knowing of the ephemeral nature of the physical form of every living being. Without exception, all physical bodies eventually fall away.

Experience the presence of the spiritual being you most trust above the crown of your head, whether it is Buddha, Jesus, Mother Mary, your guru, or simply a sphere of loving light. Open to your natural yearning to merge with the fully-awakened nature they embody— infinite love, compassion, kindness, and wisdom. Visualize that a small sphere of light in your heart center, your own awakening seed, travels upward along your spine. This sphere exits the crown of your head and comes to rest in the heart of the awakened being above you. Trust that your heart and mind has fully merged with theirs. Rest with the knowing that you are held lovingly in the heart of complete awakening.

Acknowledgements

I AM GRATEFUL TO MY WIFE AND CHILDREN for the opportunity to experience what I've written about in this book. It's a great joy and adventure. My teacher, the late Erma Pounds, was a respected friend of Hopi elders, Tibetan Buddhist teachers, and those accomplished in too many traditions to name. She was particularly adept at helping her own students cut through igo conditioning and open to awareness of our true nature. Doing so, she believed, would restore balance to people and our planet, and serve as a catalyst for the alleviation of suffering on a global scale. Thank you Erma for your life and teachings.

As an adoptive and foster parent, encountering the work of pioneering attachment psychologists has proven to be a profound gift. So many researchers and clinicians have contributed to the process of healing and wholeness for children and families. Many have also helped bridge the gap between science and contemplative spirituality by demonstrating how the cultivation of compassion and awareness benefits our brains, bodies, hearts, and minds.

The examples of His Holiness the Dalai Lama, His Holiness the Gyalwang Karmapa, and Bardor Tulku

Rinpoche as embodiments of wisdom, compassion, and awakened activity are a continual inspiration. There are several other spiritual friends to whom I am deeply grateful, Grace and Richard Yellowhammer, Patricia and Bernard DeAsis, Buddy Gatewood, Lama Palden Drolma, and Dane Larsen. Each authentically embodies the heart of their tradition—without a trace of sectarian bias—in the midst of family and community responsibilities. Thank you for your inspiring examples and friendship. Likewise, thank you to Ruth McFarland, Steve Scott, Tina Estergard, Shirlee and Doug Owen, Ambur Gore and Teddy Seman, Paul Hamilton, Randall Cutler, S.S, and so many others in the Arizona Friendship Circle and Kunzang Choling of Phoenix spiritual communities.

I deeply appreciate the enthusiasm and feedback on early drafts of this manuscript shared by my dear wife and many friends, including Caryl Ainley, Ph.D., Penelope Denton, Ph.D., Elizabeth Brazilian, Bill and Mary Glover, Ken Bacher, and Steve Larsen. I cannot thank you enough for your insights and encouragement.

And last but not least, I am grateful for the love and support of my father—the big guy who has become a mediator and meditator in his golden years—and my mother. I would not be here without your kindness.

About the Author

MICHAEL HARRIS SERVED as a journalist and analyst in the broadband industry for two decades. Through the years, his research clients have included global leaders like Verizon, Microsoft, and Samsung. He has been interviewed as an industry expert by national media and invited to present at international events. When the online information service he founded and operated was acquired by London-based United Business Media (UBM), he served as a chief analyst at UBM's *Light Reading*, the world's largest telecommunications industry publication.

Along the way, Michael travelled a journey bridging head and heart as a dharma practitioner and teacher, as well as a foster and adoptive parent. Michael served as the director of Kunzang Choling of Phoenix (KCP), a nonsectarian Buddhist center, for five years. Guided by Bardor Tulku Rinpoche, KCP is an affiliate center of Kunzang Palchen Ling (KPL) in Red Hook, NY. Michael now lives with his family in New York.

Bibliography

Mary Ainsworth, *Infancy in Uganda,* Johns Hopkins Press (1967)

Richard Bach, *Illusions: The Adventures of a Reluctant Messiah,* Dell (1989)

Francis Bacon, *Of the Proficience and Advancement of Learning, Divine and Human* (1605)

Bonnie Badenoch, *Being a Brain-Wise Therapist: A Practical Guide to Interpersonal Neurobiology,* W.W. Norton & Company (2008)

Thomas Banyacya, Address to the United Nations General Assembly, December 1992

Paul Baran, RAND Corporation, "On Distributed Communications: I. Introduction to Distributed Communications Networks," Memorandum RM-3420-PR, August 1964

Simon Baron-Cohen, *The Science of Evil: On Empathy and the Origins of Cruelty,* Basic Books (2011)

Sharon Begley, *Train Your Mind, Change Your Brain: How a New Science Reveals Our Extraordinary Potential to Transform Ourselves,* Ballantine Books (2007)

William Blake, *America a Prophecy* (1793)

David Bohm, *Changing Consciousness: Exploring the Hidden Source of the Social, Political and Environmental Crises Facing our World,* Harper (1991)

John Bowlby, "Interview with Milton Senn, MD," *Beyond the Couch: The Online Journal of the American Association for Psychoanalysis in Clinical Social Work,* Issue 2, December 2007

John Bowlby, *Maternal Care and Mental Health,* World Health Organization (1952)

Richard Bowlby and Pearl King, *Fifty Years of Attachment Theory,* Karnac Books (2004)

Britton and Gronwaldt, "Breastfeeding, Sensitivity, and Attachment," *Pediatrics,* Vol. 118, No. 5 (November 2006)

Robert Browning, *Paracelsus* (1835)

Buddhacarita, In Praise of Buddha's Acts, BDK English Tripiṭaka Series, (Taishō Vol. 4, No, 192), translated by Charles Willemen (2009)

Buddha, "Sutra of the Merit and Virtue of the Past Vows of Medicine Master Vaidurya Light Tathágata," Buddhist Text Translation Society, (1997)

E.A. Burbank, *Burbank Among the Indians*, Caxton Press (1944, 1972)

Joanna Carey, "Who Hasn't Met Harry?" *The Guardian*, February 16, 1999

Joseph Campbell and Bill Moyers, *The Power of Myth*, Anchor (1991)

Joseph Campbell, *The Hero with a Thousand Faces*, New World Library (2008)

Pema Chödrön, "Bodhichitta: The Excellence of Awakened Heart," *Shambhala Sun*, September 2001

Condon, Desbordes, Miller, DeSteno, "Meditation Increases Compassionate Responses to Suffering," *Psychological Science* (2013)

Crittenden, Partridge, & Claussen, "Family Patterns of Relationship in Normative and Dysfunctional Families," *Development and Psychopathology*, Vol. 3, Issue 4, p.491-512 (1991)

The Dalai Lama, *Freedom in Exile: The Autobiography of the Dalai Lama,* HarperCollins (1991)

The Dalai Lama, Nicholas Vreeland, *An Open Heart: Practicing Compassion in Everyday Life*, Little, Brown, (2008)

Richard Davidson, "Transform Your Mind, Change Your Brain," Google Tech Talk, September 23, 2009

Pierre Teilhard de Chardin, *The Phenomenon of Man* (1955)

Antoine de Saint-Exupéry, *The Little Prince*, Mariner Books (2000)

DYI and Zero to Three "What Grown-Ups Understand About Child Development: A National Benchmark Survey" (2000)

Michael Dieperink, et al, "Attachment Style Classification and Posttraumatic Stress Disorder in Former Prisoners of War," *American Journal of Orthopsychiatry*, Volume 71, Issue 3, July 2001, p.374–378

Davey du Plessis, "Thank You," October 17, 2012, blog accessed at www.daveyduplessis.com/blog/thank-you

Bibliography

Naomi I. Eisenberger, Matthew D. Lieberman, Kipling D. Williams, "Does Rejection Hurt? An fMRI Study of Social Exclusion," *Science*, Vol. 302, October 10, 2003

Thomas Stearns Eliot, *The Cocktail Party: A Comedy*, Samuel French, Inc. (1978)

Dan Evehema, "A Hopi Elder Speaks," *The Open Line*, Volume 14, Issue 12 (2000)

R. Douglas Field, "White Matter Matters," *Scientific American*, March 2008, p.54–61

Barbara L. Fredrickson, et al, "A Functional Genomic Perspective on Human Well-Being," *Proceedings of the National Academy of Sciences*, Vol. 110, No. 33 (August 2013)

Omri Gillath, Phillip R. Shaver, Mario Mikulincer, "An Attachment-Theoretical Approach to Compassion and Altruism," in *Compassion: Its Nature and Use in Psychotherapy*, P. Gilbert (2005)

Vivette Glover, "Annual Research Review: Prenatal Stress and the Origins of Psychopathology: an Evolutionary Perspective," *Journal of Child Psychology and Psychiatry*, Volume 52, Issue 4, p.356–367, April 2011

Daniel Goleman, *Social Intelligence: The New Science of Human Relationships*, Random House (2006)

Peter Gray, "Freedom to Learn: The Roles of Play and Curiosity as Foundations for Learning," *Psychology Today*, July 9, 2009

Hartesveldt and Harvey, "The Fire Ecology of Sequoia Regeneration," Tall Timbers Fire Ecology Conference (1967)

Donald Olding Hebb, *The Organization of Behavior: A Neuropsychological Theory*, Wiley (1949)

Jeremy Holmes, *John Bowlby and Attachment Theory,* Psychology Press (1993)

Hölzelemail, Carmody, Vangel, Congleton, Yerramsetti, Gard, Lazar, "Mindfulness Practice Leads to Increases in Regional Brain Gray Matter Density," *Psychiatry Research: Neuroimaging*, Vol. 191, Issue 1, p.36–43, January 30, 2011

William James, *The Principles of Psychology*, Volume 1, H. Holt (1905)

William James, *The Varieties of Religious Experience: A Study in Human Nature* (1902)

Carl Gustav Jung, *Memories, Dreams, Reflections*, Random House (1989)

Jon Kabat-Zinn, *Wherever You Go, There You Are: Mindfulness Meditation in Everyday Life*, Hyperion (2009)

Kahan, Jenkins-Smith, and Braman, "Cultural Cognition of Scientific Consensus," *Journal of Risk Research*, Vol. 14, p.147-74, 2011

The Karmapa Ogyen Trinley Dorje, *The Heart Is Noble: Changing the World from the Inside Out*, Shambhala (February 2013)

Dan Katchongva, "From the Beginning of Life to the Day of Purification Teachings, History & Prophecies of the Hopi," Committee for Traditional Indian Land and Life, Los Angeles, California (1972)

Laozi, Stephen Mitchell, *Tao Te Ching: A New English Version*, HarperCollins (1988)

Sara W. Lazar, et al., "Meditation Experience is Associated with Increased Cortical Thickness," *Neuroreport* 16(17), November 28, 2005

J. C. R. Licklider, "Memorandum for Members and Affiliates of the Intergalactic Computer Network," April 23, 1963

Paul Linden, *Winning is Healing: Body Awareness and Empowerment For Abuse Survivors*, CCMS Publications (2006)

Keller, Litzelman, Wisk, et al, "Does the Perception that Stress Affects Health Matter? The Association with Health and Mortality," *Health Psychology*, American Psychological Association, September 2012, 31(5), p.677-684

Abraham Maslow, *Motivation and Personality*, Harper (1954)

Abraham Maslow, "Personality Problems and Personality Growth," in *The Self: Explorations in Personal Growth* (1956)

William McDougall, *An Introduction to Social Psychology*, Methuen & Co. (1908)

Iain McGhilchrist, *The Master and His Emissary: The Divided Brain and the Making of the Western World*, Yale University Press (2010)

Michael J. Meaney, "Epigenetics and the Biological Definition of Gene," *Child Development*, January/February 2010, Vol. 81, Number 1, p. 41–79

Jamgon Mipham, *White Lotus: An Explanation of the Seven-line Prayer to Guru Padmasambhava*, Shambhala (2007)

Erin M. Myers, Virgil Zeigler-Hill, "How Much Do Narcissists Really Like Themselves? Using the Bogus Pipeline Procedure to Better Understand the Self-Esteem of Narcissists,"

Journal of Research in Personality, Vol. 46 (2012), p.102–105

NIH, NICHD, *The NICHD Study of Early Child Care and Youth Development: Findings for children up to age 4½ years*. NIH Pub. No. 05-4318 (January 2006).

Norman & Shallice, "Attention to Action: Willed and Automatic Control of Behavior," in *Cognitive Neuroscience: A Reader* (1991), by Michael S. Gazzaniga (Oxford: Blackwell)

Christiane Northrup, *Women's Bodies, Women's Wisdom*, Bantam (2010)

John O'Donohue, *Anam Cara: A Book of Celtic Wisdom,* Harper-Collins (1998)

Don Alejandro Cirilo Perez Oxlaj, personal conversation with author in Tikal, Guatemala, May 2006, translated to English by Elizabeth Araujo

Padmasambhava, Marcia Binder Schmidt, Erik Pema Kunsang, *Dzogchen Essentials: The Path that Clarifies Confusion*, Rangjung Yeshe Publications (2004)

Padmasambhava, *Treasures from Juniper Ridge*, Rangjung Yeshe Publications (2008)

M. Scott Peck, *People of the Lie: The Hope for Healing Human Evil*, Touchstone (1998)

M. Scott Peck, *The Road Less Traveled: A New Psychology of Love, Traditional Values and Spiritual Growth,* Touchstone (2003)

David M. Perlman, Tim V. Salomons, Richard J. Davidson, Antoine Lutz, "Differential Effects on Pain Intensity and Unpleasantness of Two Meditation Practices," *Emotion*, 2010, Vol. 10, No. 1, p.65–71, American Psychological Association

Robyn L. Powers, David J. Marks, et al, "Stimulant Treatment in Children with Attention-Deficit/Hyperactivity Disorder Moderates Adolescent Academic Outcome," *Journal of Child and Adolescent Psychopharmacology*, 18(5), p.449–459, October 2008

Jane Qiu, "China: The Third Pole," *Nature*, July 2008

Reddy, Negi, Dodson-Lavelle, Ozawa-de Silva, Pace, Cole, Raison, Craighead, "Engagement with Cognitively-Based Compassion Training is Associated with Reduced Salivary C-reactive Protein from Before to After Training in Foster Care Program Adolescents," *Psychoneuroendocrinology*, 10.1016 (2012)

Reddy, Negi, Dodson-Lavelle, Ozawa-de Silva, Pace, Cole, Raison, Craighead, "Cognitive-Based Compassion Training: A Promising Prevention Strategy for At-Risk Adolescents," *Journal of Child and Family Studies* 10.1007 (2012)

Edwin F. Renaud, "The Attachment Characteristics of Combat Veterans with PTSD," *Traumatology*, Volume 14, No. 3 (September 2008)

Bardor Tulku Rinpoche, teaching in Phoenix, Arizona, translated by Yeshe Gyamtso (2012)

Khenchen Thrangu Rinpoche, Erik Pema Kunsang, *Songs of Naropa: Commentaries on Songs of Realization*, Rangjung Yeshe Publications (1997)

Tulku Urgyen Rinpoche, *Blazing Splendor: The Memoirs of Tulku Urgyen Rinpoche*, North Atlantic Books (2005), Daniel Goleman (Introduction)

Yongey Mingyur Rinpoche, "Beyond Meditation," *Shambhala Sun*, September 2010

J.K. Rowling, *Harry Potter and the Sorcerer's Stone,* Scholastic (1998)

J. K. Rowling, *Harry Potter and the Prisoner of Azkaban*, Large Print Press (1999)

J.K. Rowling, *Harry Potter and the Order of the Phoenix,* Thorndike Press (2003)

Steve Roth, "Stories of His Holiness the 16th Karmapa," Chögyam Trungpa Chronicle Project (July 17, 2010)

Mary Salter, "An Evaluation of Adjustment Based on the Concept of Security," (Ph.D. dissertation, University of Toronto, 1940)

Allan N. Schore, *Affect Regulation and the Repair of the Self*, W. W. Norton & Company (2003)

Allan N. Schore, "Attachment and the Regulation of the Right Brain," *Attachment & Human Development* Vol. 2, No 1 (April 2000), p.23–47

Schuengel, Jzendoorn, Bakermans-Kranenburg, "Disorganized Attachment in Early Childhood: Meta-analysis of Precursors, Concomitants, and Sequelae," *Development and Psychopathology*, 11 (1999), p.225–249

Peter M. Senge, C. Otto Scharmer, Joseph Jaworski, Betty S., Flowers, *Presence: An Exploration of Profound Change in People, Organizations and Society*, Random House (2005)

Bibliography

Shantideva, *The Way of the Bodhisattva*, translated by Adam Pearcey, Rigpa Translations (2007)

Jack P. Shonkoff, Deborah Phillips, *From Neurons to Neighborhoods: The Science of Early Childhood Development*, National Academies Press (2000)

Jack P. Shonkoff, AS Garner, Committee on Psychosocial Aspects of Child and Family Health; Committee on Early Childhood, Adoption, and Dependent Care; Section on Developmental and Behavioral Pediatrics, "The Lifelong Effects of Early Childhood Adversity and Toxic Stress," *Pediatrics*, January 2012, 129(1), p.232-46

Daniel J. Siegel, *Developing Mind, Second Edition: How Relationships and the Brain Interact to Shape Who We Are*, Guilford Press (2012)

Daniel J. Siegel, *Mindsight: The New Science of Personal Transformation*, Bantam (2009)

Bruce D. Smith, "The Initial Domestication of Cucurbita Pepo in the Americas 10,000 Years Ago," *Science*, May 1997, Vol. 276, Issue 5314, p.932-934

Marion Solomon and Stan Tatkin, *Love and War in Intimate Relationships: Connection, Disconnection, and Mutual Recognition in Couple Therapy,* W. W. Norton & Company (2011)

Sroufe, Egland, Carlson, Collins, *The Development of the Person: The Minnesota Study of Risk and Adaptation from Birth to Adulthood*, Guilford Publications (2005)

L. Alan Sroufe, "Ritalin Gone Wrong," *The New York Times*, January 28, 2012

Rolf Alfred Stein, *Tibetan Civilization*, Stanford University Press (1972)

Jampa Mackenzie Stewart, *The Life of Gampopa,* Snow Lion Publications (2004)

Elizabeth Marshall Thomas, *The Old Way: A Story of the First People*, Macmillan (2007)

Tilopa, "Pith Instructions on Mahamudra," translated by Ken McLeod

Tilopa, "Six Words of Advice," translated by Ken McLeod

Chögyam Trungpa, John Baker, Marvin Casper, *The Myth of Freedom and The Way of Meditation*, Shambhala Publications (2005)

Heruka Tsangnyon, Andrew Quintman, Donald S. Lopez, Jr., *The Life of Milarepa*, Penguin (2010)

Yeshe Tsogyal, *The Lotus-Born: The Life Story of Padmasambhava*, Rangjung Yeshe Publications (2004)

Abraham J. Twerski, *Addictive Thinking: Understanding Self-Deception*, Hazelden Publishing (1997)

U.S. Federal Civil Defense Administration, *Duck and Cover* (1952)

Lilly Wachowski and Lana Wachowski, *The Matrix,* Warner Bros. (1999)

David J. Wallin, *Attachment in Psychotherapy,* Guilford Press (2007)

Glenn Wallis, "Bhavana: A Guide to Classical Buddhist Meditation" (2009)

Victor Walsh and Gerald Golins, "The Outward Bound Process Model" (1976)

Yangemail and Raine, "Prefrontal Structural and Functional Brain Imaging Findings in Antisocial, Violent, and Psychopathic Individuals: A Meta-analysis," *Psychiatry Research: Neuroimaging*, Vol. 174, Issue 2, p.81–88, November 30, 2009

Paramahansa Yogananda, *Autobiography of a Yogi,* Self-Realization Fellowship (1998)

Zhuang Zi, Chuang Tzu, Derek Bryce, *Nan-Hua-Ch'En-Ching: The Treatise of the Transcendent Master from Nan-Hu*, Llanerch Press (1995)